# Alstonefield: a poem

PETER RILEY was born in 1940 near Manchester. He studied at Pembroke College, Cambridge and the universities of Keele and Sussex. He has taught at the University of Odense (Denmark), and since 1975 has lived as a freelance writer, English teacher and bookseller. He lived for ten years in the Peak District and is now based in Cambridge, with regular sojourns in Transylvania and elsewhere.

Also by Peter Riley from Carcanet

*Passing Measures*

# PETER RILEY

## *Alstonefield*

a poem

CARCANET

# Acknowledgements

Two and a half lines of the seventeenth stanza are by Helen Macdonald. Most of the twenty-fifth stanza (the first complete stanza of Part III) is after André du Bouchet.

An earlier version of Parts I to IV of the poem was published by Oasis Books and Shearsman Books (Ian Robinson and Tony Frazer) in 1995 under the title *Alstonefield*. A section of Part V was published as issue 41 of *Shearsman* entitled 'Hilltop Episode' (1998); other passages have appeared in *Salt*, *Involution*, and *Gare du Nord*.

First published in Great Britain in 2003 by
Carcanet Press Limited
Alliance House
Cross Street
Manchester M2 7AQ

A CIP catalogue record for this book is available from the British Library
ISBN 1 85754 648 2

The publisher acknowledges financial assistance from Arts Council England

Typeset in Monotype Garamond by XL Publishing Services, Tiverton
Printed and bound in England by SRP Ltd, Exeter

Alstonefield, sometimes spelled Alstonfield, is a limestone village in North Staffordshire at OS grid reference SK132556, on high ground between the valleys of the rivers Dove and Manifold, close to the west edge of the former. Almost all the local place-names in the poem are in its vicinity, within a radius of about three miles, mainly to the north of the village. Geologically this area is close to the western edge of a dome of carboniferous limestone about twelve miles across, cut into by stream and river valleys, called the Peak District.

# Contents

Preface                    1

*Alstonefield: a poem*
Part I                     5
Part II                    9
Part III                  15
Part IV                   20
Part V                    23

Notes                    103

# Preface

*Excerpts from two letters to Tony Baker*

## 1

6th August 1991

Dear Tony,

[...] speaking of which, on the way back from Liverpool last time
we stopped for the night at Alstonefield, and as I was strolling
among the fields south of the village in the evening I suddenly had
the distinct sensation that it mattered, this place, that its very exis-
tence mattered. I surprised myself, because obviously there's
nothing there that any version of cultural modernity needs for half
a second. Limestone hills, sheep pasturage, meandering river dales
– what does any contemporary claim want with any of it? Yet there
it was, all round me, manifestly necessary. I was amazed. As you
know, I lived nearby for four years so I should have known, but
everyday sights do diminish so, don't you think, and sink to
marginal residues of our upkeep, if we don't have a theology to
polish them with.

And I began to think of the place as an arena, a theatre of outra-
geously manipulated light in which the soul puts on a show for the
people, where the self's instant of being is depicted as the lost
masquer bearing a lantern among towering land-forms, in search
of his company. I could see that it would be necessary to enter this
scene again and again in search of the plot, threading questions
and trials into the labyrinth, the complex displays of rock and
vegetation, sheep-pens and graveyards, set up by the masters of
the challenge, the pluralities that devised this spectacle and left it

1

there like an open book. And a writing was needed, an interlinear commentary, to work the self through the fairground of its purpose and throw a shadow image back to all the rest of the known.

It had to be like that, it had to be a performance, because there was no trace of those pure and simple instruments with which we wage our self-wars, like 'nature' or 'society', and the human mental heart seemed to be cast before the eyes as an unhoused proposal, a thing of many possible directions, carrying everywhere on its back a balancing or compensating device which always begs to differ, always seeks the exception. For nothing up there is quite itself, everything bears the shadow of its contrary. An upland pastoral community run by machines; a weekend break zone for the wild soul which betrays refused planning permission at every turn; sublimity locked into sordidness on the high pastures, elegance and care struggling with cynical exploitation in the valleys... It finally seemed, set there in the centre of England, the very literature of what people are, the star-wars shooting round anyone's living-room in Bradford. Am I rambling? I hope so.

The manic 'Estimate' Brown, you will recall, stopped at Dovedale on his way to Keswick and hated the place – shrivelled valleys, miniature grandeur, he said, the horror without the sublimity or the immensity; meaning it was separated from 'society' without offering that surrender of the wild self into its full theatrical suicide as of the Lakes or the moors above Haworth. It wasn't simple and it wasn't enough – it was halfway there, it was untidy. Well I don't know, I adore all that surface water further north, the constancy of the music, but I've lived through enough manifestos and I've begun to believe in peace, messy and running-failed as it is, the blank horror these states face at the prospect of having to live without an enemy. And anyway, that segmented limestone dome ringed in darkness (ringed in squalor, actually, and waste) cuts natural light into the most 'untoward thoughts' without any help from theoretical Marxism.

And since we no longer have to give personal names to the entities that debate within the arts of perception, the articulation is less socially predicated – I like that. To stay with landscape objects and chunks of thought, like living in one of Ben Nicholson's paintings, and our entire traffic is set a questionnaire, concerning worth and tenure, which I thought could be played as a continuity impelled by hidden reserves, like the Irish bagpipes, without any, or much, sparring against the Kleptocracy being needed, and certainly not to have to ape the kind of de-relating *coupure* you get in *The News* visuals.

[…] the slender fit of grey stone buildings and dry-stone walls into a very diverse ground of curved grey-green slopes – at every turn spreading outwards, the edges of the view streaked with white lines always curving upwards to a provisional horizon […] particularly as it was twilight, and the moon was large in a clear sky so all the near fields were silvered into a texture like the gloss of human skin… And the pub is a good place for a cheap meal for the wandering, and suitably impoverished, definitely proletarian, pastoral or pasteurised, writing person, at the end of a day.

We must take a walk there some time.

**2**

10th February 1993

[…]
I keep going back. It's still there, every time. I stay in a B & B in the village and moon around the landscape, sometimes alone, sometimes I bring someone with me. I don't write, I don't carry notebooks; I walk in the valleys, I stand in the fields, until I get home. I'm making sure it's still there – 'it' being not exactly Alstonefield but the challenge and serenity it conveys, and for that there's no alternative but to be there, there's no channel of information in the world I could trust. If someone comes with me I listen carefully to the same scene working through a different life, until the person becomes a term and extension of my own meditation, and a question and exit. So there are also matters raised not mine, and not settled by anything I know, which have to be entrusted to the language as to the hills clothed in weather. And can be, for this tactic also discloses the limits of personal poetry. An enormous fight starts between 'the' and 'a' which tenses the entire discourse: traditional stagecraft versus objectivist texte. As

yet inconclusive, unfinished, and I'm increasingly unsure which side I'm on, whether the world can be captured in a small ring, or should be left to its natural dissipation in detail.

The house I usually stay in has a very 1930s feel, especially about the windows with cast-iron radiators beneath them, bay windows with small panels that let in a lot of daylight and look out onto pasture marked out by dry limestone walls, modest heights mostly implicit in the distant folds of grey-green which can prove quite formidable when you actually visit them. The whole landscape is fixed under a geometry of stone walls, parallelograms and asymptotic curves charting all the wave-like thrusts. I seem to breathe a pre-war atmosphere known from poetry, fiction, film, or the generations remembering – a theatre of pauses, dream hotels and branch-line halts, a roller-coaster of green roads, calm metrics ruled over depression and despair, a working industrial city beyond the hills forming its new image of man, Nash visions of eternity sitting quietly on the grass, a literary tramp at leisure in every barn and haystack... It was the period that bore me, which everyone always remembered with affection: 'The war put an end to all that', whatever it was, it's difficult to say. It lived in the country hotel as in the Marxist meeting above the taproom. Something was held in the hand which meant something. Stability and change as coextensive, a central healing balance between the cruelties of monetarist disdain and those of underdog resentment. So a hope. The war put an end to it. But it sits for me unrecognised in those dull fields like a Chinese poem, a spirit flight distilled to leaf patience. A deific glow that scutters out of sight when you turn to face it, but integral to the entire geology. Because it is a sedimentary landscape, however distorted in the details of the disrupted surface: the horizontal successions of settling fundamentals underpin everything you see, layer upon layer.

By the time I get there it's usually getting dark. I install myself, go to the inn for dinner, and then wander over to the churchyard. Which is a rather obvious prosodic gesture, but everyone needs help getting started.

Well, we didn't get that walk in yet.

Love to all, P.

# I

Again the figured curtain draws across the sky.
Daylight shrinks, clinging to the stone walls
and rows of graveyard tablets, the moon rising
over the tumbling peneplain donates some equity
to the charter and the day's accountant
stands among tombs, where courtesy dwells.
Thus a special and slight enclosure is set,
slight as the dark spaces I fill tonight and
silent and motionless as lives become, swelling
with truth, scattered with glowing plaques.


Darkness opens the sky to space. Fallen
light sets up its booth in the stoneyard
where the theatre of eyes flickers and dies.
The moon sails the eastern sky, rides
the upland fields in sole possession,
the scattered runs of grey wall the walled
yard and the speaking stones, that say there is
something made in a life not to be lost
however small it is not to be crossed,
not to be cast in sightless wax.

But is kept folded in this unvalued space,
space free of us, where the moon slices time.
Void of us, where we didn't take any
advantage but sailed away, leaving
old bones kicked around the churchyard
and carried off by dogs and wrote out
the only true thing we are, a record
of love. Every impossible meeting
happens here in darkness and silence
and the slightness of the piecing mind.


A beautiful thing, the moon on stone, and
central. In a momentary breeze the trees
sway slightly and clap over the churchyard,
patches of hawthorn and yew claiming some
marginal light part towards the edge
leaving the moon's direct file on old names.
A farewell to the world that opens the world
and sets standards of dealing. How
could you secretise the language on this
final stage or place a reserve on hope


When the world is watching you? Mirror flashes
on the horizon, distances steeped in petrol,
lives snapped to zero across thronging waste and
planning ethnic cleansing in Mansfield. Death
pressed through the dream into constant
separation as the waking world coats itself
in speed, factorial of despair, that
defeats the bearer absolutely wall to wall:
the action without cause, the daylight caves.
We turn our backs, only the night is kind.

Of course we turn our backs, what is there
to speak through the coils of resentment
but denial, heart loss across the mirror
that coats the bank, what is claimed but self?
I retire to a distance, I have the right
in the late evening and on through the dark hours
keeping to the edge of the necessary plot:
trade, marriage, maintenance, the sacred cast
of continuance always at risk, fixed with loss,
moon marks on stone, trenching the calendar.


I thought I heard in the still night air
a mother suckling her babe and singing
softly in the darkness: Poor little mite,
the cruel captains of earth will wrest
thy virtue to their standing in spite,
and all of thy trust in good will
have to find its own way to the centre
without me, who am not there. Poor
accidental thing, she said, poor rabbit,
what ardour you bear to an unknown point.


Her milk was blue in the sky, it was
time to go. The moon like a knife in water
slid silently down the firmament and sank
into the trees and hedges, shaking themselves
in the dawn wind. The question frames
the response in emergent green: my life
may be kept in some spare cupboard as
needed from time to time or not but the light
spread again through the grass stalks
and the flesh trembled in its window.

I must be blind, to see such brightness
in such delicate light, to see the world
in its hope as a leaf turns in the
movement of cool air a memory trace
sufficient to keep a name in stone,
the letters full of moss. I would serve
for ever the few ecstasies that form
such a purpose, the child's space at
the table, anger stretching into the future,
obedience glowing at every joint.

# II

'The sky will not help you, the soil and trees
will not help you, to die in peace.' So don't,
carry your account and rankle with the fox
in the valley, ever on the loose under
the chains of despair, ever alert to
the movements of the gentle victim
we know well, the soft breathing
in the wooden box, the leaps of inspace,
we know the lamb. Whose anger paces
out in the stone day and crests the end.

And know at evening when a path
to the heart opens for the cold and
dark airs of the earth full of locked spirits
and disputed graves. The light bows and
turns its back on the receding uplands
coated in false frost, the hill crests take
the surge of territory to its break and
mark it as on paper, ink under blue wash.
Making clear what I thought I knew, that
truth is at the rim and rings like cash.

At the rim of land is a return of knowledge,
spilling from the lip. Several pages of worked
time graft my trust to this fair lecture as
the staves ring out. Secured in the reprieve,
balm and fescue stretch to the succeeding line.
What it means is that I might have done nothing
but help a different sight into the world and
wouldn't that be something, wouldn't the graves
smoke in the small hours to bear such a legend?
'He spoke to us and it was safe to continue.'


A sight not mine I mean. The fields are dark
and the sheep with their long ears are alert
in the night, where we purchased the wine,
of separation and took it at the rim where
the bubbles winked. You were with me
though you may now forget, how safe it was
to take affection under the wing entirely
and trust it the whole length of the dark road.
The bulk of love obstructs all my fantasy.
Calm the lamb sleeps its future.


How can anyone believe solo the very idea
mocks itself. Day closes from the start on this
limestone chessboard and today the autumn sun
smote the western sides of the tall grass stalks
and lowered gradually until the cream of being
shone back and then it was total, all colours
clenched in grey-white over the hill's back it was
the rose of time in the earth pocket. Fear it
continuously, is how I came to know the spectral
city in the end, all the way back to the B & B.

Now I sleep in Alstonefield. Gods and goddesses
walk in the dark fields and stand in a ring in the
churchyard waiting for light. Of which I have it all
over my pillow alone except the permanent.
Gradually in the wine of sleep a completed memory
compassed by care makes a globe of love. Very
little I can do with it, alone. But it is like
a repair depôt that continues through governments
and wars at the end of a small back road where
carefree labourers stroll around dark and competent.


As any night. Looking out of my window at
dawn the voice of desire is raucous but filial
because of the narrow gap containing the
river invisible from here. There the war is
final and formal, where gods and goddesses
enter their own. The fields coated in water
do everything to light the mind can bear
except block it like a town. I think my
dressing gown is a thin and crucial history
of lads and lasses up to good before my time.


In the days of pink-toes I lived down the road.
I picked boletus in the woods, effed around the
local employment situation and drank a daily
bout of distance marked in infant years.
It was my wine to rest by the stone wall at
summer's end far from Cambridge, where
cthonic severance dictates endless toil.
When a meticulous light brought a sequence
of detail to sever the intimate, I thought
to trust the gloss on the stem of travail.

Now the narrow breakfast while the world
stands outside garmented in fall, the plunge
and stay of the valley sides, limestone edges
scrubbed to a gloss and shedding soil.
Garlands hang on the outer door
and the voice is clenched, saying there is never
enough passed on, the body substantiates
only its own and when the sun returns
the day is closed for the night. Here my life
turns to the earth, and peers into the pit.


Hanging on Thor's lip, the whirlpool cave
hung over the valley while the miner's hammer
sounds traces of enriched water to an under-
ground palace shining with promises. Take
what's available and depart: a gentlemanly
mode in the bed of state. I don't blame you
for running love against profit, O lubric self,
but I know the victim well. I know the sore
throat, the scratched palm, the sleeping bag
in the shop doorway. I hear the passing bell.


It rings, and the throat opens into song
as a matrix clutching the future across
fallen cloud, seeking a long friendship.
Then another day draws to a close and the
restless pastures seem to suck light
into themselves as if nothing human had
any right to it, they say, make yourselves
gods and better, or leave it alone, leave
the light out of your dark passages for good.
Do you remember Lulu and April Fever?

I remember nothing but a trace of soul
difficult to specify now in the rush
of weeks. Not quite finished, the day pulls
hard towards Stoke and gets us to the
George Inn. The food is good and cheap
the mild is strong and the hope is of
worthiness, possibly too as I walk back
finger inter finger with you on the dark road
each in performance integral, are we. I trust so.
The dark is deeper when the trust is stronger.


In the night it rains. In the tight bed
I am an earth feature witnessing a sublime
artefact. And someone in the other room
dreams language to a stone, a white
silence breaking the skin, like a mother
nursing absence as the rain on the window
wipes pretence and claim. A persistent singing
pierces the cloudy distance – tightly
bound as I am, taut as a harp in the
autumnal cyclone, I want your rest.


And nourish my fate, with little to
grow or be faithful to but what's already
counted, and set aside. I note in the night
the messengers at the window, bringing
our emanations to the edge of peace where
our bodies writhe nightly against time,
tense for birth, answer or final clause. But
I'll pack you a sandwich tomorrow if I may
and we'll take it out to the high woods
and watch the godly insects making laws.

To this purpose wake, the sun is high
and the fields are white, not exactly
white but it has snowed. The fields are
different.

# III

And the voice is broken before
the alterior face, the future is cast open
on the page. For a fideism of the heart, oh
what pastoral thing is that, what rich red
and blue border. The vastness of love is cut
to a small song out in the wild closet.
I wrap my neck, collect a frozen stone.


The mountain edge barely clears, folded back.
Surface that is a line hanging in the air
at which sight withdraws, a clarity on paper
anterior to the earth, broken by ink.
Lines that converge without touching
open centrally to a linen distance,
the whole air a time table. Light from
the blade retires behind the hill at
a slight flexing of the globe as the words
I thought this with fly to your calvarium.


I walk back to Beresford in the afternoon.
The coal tit, dyed in modern philosophy,
flits for nuts. Snow on the shoulder, sky
narrowed between hill and hill a blue-grey
tongue whose speech is far from here.
Silence lines the horizon, glowing like a lost
nation, snow-brushed fields glossing the vein
to a hole in tense, a history of light, or, moving
pain to paper an agreement is touched,
that death shall have no choice.

Clouds of pale ash drift over from
the big world, smearing the spread blades
with urban dereliction, a monosyllable
atomised on the screen to narrative, tales
of renewed vigour and washing foam.
Reception is difficult in the hills
but we make shift, erect stringy masts
on shed roofs over the moors, send our boys
out gleaming white and wash our hands again
and again and again, having no choice.


Walton's lodge is just visible through the trees
and bushes on the other side of the river,
cream stone pilasters, monument to patience
where the river turns and enters at a tangent
a more demanding geology. And holds the light
on its surface closely argued at the bend a
systemic grammar, I mean a sort of canopy
protecting the delicate under of the human leaf
from dark dividedness or fallen ardour. Walton's
lodge is just visible through bushes and trees.


As in the oval meadow the light is gathered
such as it is in February abstract and alone:
self-supporting, concentric economy comprising
substantially the reach of language, which
is slight, and delicately toned. Toned, that
is, with failure and decay as air enters the
surface of things in late winter and light
harbours in water, a contractual figure or in-
telligence. Bow to it and cross the glowing river
on a wooden footbridge into fast-land.

As in that oval meadow, there is a light
that stands apart, without colour for it has no aim,
a pastoral substantive where the story gathers
to a close and the community accedes to what
'must be' in secret delight. Here the maidens
dance on the darkening green to the end of day,
a torse in history that rights itself by
candle lanterns, as the soul is timed to
exequies. Bow to it and cross the glowing river
on a wooden footbridge into urban despair.


As in that oval meadow the deities are slight,
their energy spreads from cliff to river and
in that circumference stands, white on white,
a silent hammer, an arch in the air, the wind
blows through it. Cosmic history in the metaphrase
of sexual reticence, but when a text belongs to
its addressee there is that opening of the heart
and finding a ring inside it, and/or a stone.
Nod to it and cross the doubled, shining river
on a wooden footbridge into prose.


As in that oval meadow I cannot speak. Shadows
of the edging trees band the lawn that upcurves
so slightly at the pericarp or tone border I
am head-bashed against the fact of my ardour:
love takes no reason, answers no call, stands
sufficient in the light it is to bypass its
bearer and wake a line through generation,
a blindness viewing an unborn shade.
Obey to it and walk on the stone slabs of
a wooden footbridge into semblance.

So, poetry, grey chemicals on the grass
an abandoned centre which is where
we live, I and I. The price increases as the
light fails, without substantive rights
the money is a vapour on the screen wherever
it clings, the nation vanishing at its edge.
And certainly there are people in the towns,
possibly there are ghosts in the caves and
certain voices crowd me along the valley base
I walk alone in the colder and colder fade.


The cold is resistible, the news is a knife held
aloft by an over-heated person shouting Down
with bourgeois individualism. I resist it and sweat
uphill to Alstonefield, sinking with night into the
George Inn with chicken and chips, mild and
Jamesons surrounded by talk, talking the world
into a biological shroud on the mind, doing
fine, having a good time, making news tonight.
The fire burns within, the owls hoot out
in the cold I am a happy lapsing overdraw


From which the heart has departed and glides
winged over the smouldering developments.
And walk back alone between dark snowy fields
where the long-eared sheep are ever alert
and the groaning wood. I grasp an absent hand,
finger inter finger, I call it Impossibility.
And impossibility is a sweet sleep I owe
myself in a house among big trees, a wine of
world-light swirling in the skull, touching
neuter again at some pain, without any loss.

To rise to blinding light flooding
the breakfast salon and the distance
to Buxton, where there's a book fair.
I don't know why I bother. Anyone
can hear it in the skin response, and
raise a pale glass.

## IV

            Important to
check every visit that certain places
are still intact, haven't been more than
sense can stand eroded by desubstantiating
forces known collectively as shopping. More


Or less they survive: Beresford Dale and upper
Wolfscote, somewhat Santa's Grotto now with
the new walkers' autobahn and though no one who
hadn't lived here would notice, trimmings.
Then the Manifold from the Mill to Thor's Cave
returning to the blanched uplands round Wetton
and Alstonefield where the landlady finds me
puzzling, keeps coming back here in
different company and can't work out what's
going on: Ewan, Helen, Beryl, or no one at all.


One day I'll get Lorand Gaspar up here
or Voichitsa Tepei or the unfractured self.
Driving past Harecops with you the stresses
are few and distinct, three or four to a line,
major choices in a life, like crucifixes on alpine
passes marking breaks and meetings across
hung ground. Where lives converge, and central
vaccua aligned are the birth graves of gods.
The old stone house stands firm in its measure
grass to the door and the washing ensign aloft.

Blue hills later in the photograph that weren't
ever blue, cold feet in the bed, a true
record is a desperate thing. Indeed we are
you and I finished the moment it speaks and
lie in the village graveyard attracting
rare names from the night sky. They close
in on our plot while we sleep through the
local accommodation, night full of stones
eyes closed dark admonition serious message
your breath my script scripted burthen meant.


Ever. Serious message get on with your business.
Which is to be here in all kinds of weathers
and walk and walking trade my pulse for
notices of souldom in geophysical latitude
spurning the news. The politics of this
carries hope like a feather on the palm:
my country tracks are crossed in oil and
its inhering slaughter. The oval meadow
trusts minds only, the broken ring-dance
humanises permanent assets to the world.


Heavens it dwells so in the hand that
might one evening grasp an opportunity
and so create warfare as the small centre
swells into speculation. The slightest
disclosure of the heart tracks a host
out of hiding and waves bright banners
north to south of power, where amor
lies broken and divided. Recumbent light
on the wind stretcher, a field of
dandelion clocks, header into goal.

Green hills why did your power abstain?
and the wrapping mafiosi cash the
benign influences at the Westminster –
I'd risk alcoholic poisoning to know, or
the big starchy dinners at the George Inn
night after night but nothing tells me this.
Where lives converge we abjure power and so
advantages can be taken and of course are.
I find walking back to the B & B with my
wife on my arm the god-grounds are equable.


We walk and talk and little notice how
some recent grasp has thinned the pasture
until the invasion is complete. But look
how the non-human belongs, how the bones of
the landscape trellis the darkness, how nothing
intervenes between the eye and its home.
Then we must be more than a condition,
a crown in hiding, a burning shade. I find
walking back to the guest house with my
companion to hand the god tracks converge.


So by the walls of grey houses with
small windows some lit in the night that
stand there like gravestones century after
century and individuals and families pass
through them and out, each making a more
or less hearted wrapper of the inside some-
thing tells me that nothing is gained but
a vulnerable honesty bidded against death.
I find walking back to where I sleep with my
teacher the heart light is shielded.

# V

Another damp Sunday morning, up and walk over
Pea Low (another distressed tumulus) and what's that
flicker in the distance? What's that convergence west
of the village? And why are the roads so busy this
English morning? Petrol flips the work-day whip
and we poor peasants dive for the verge. Binoculars.
A curlew calls far and long falling as I focus
on the fact. Cut short the walk, curve under
Gratton Hill and back down – the battle's up:
it's that trough in time, it's a car boot sale!


It is difficult to know the good in lives.
If I'd found a rare object I might have gone
chirruping to Stoke in the pouring rain
which threatens. Dull English weather,
the day stands inert, colour stops dead,
distance diffused, a green field and a shed
with the usual water tank at the back of a farm
in the mud. It would be specious to pretend
that any bit of British countryside is anything
but an agricultural factory marked Piss Off.

And people open their car boots to reveal
image destitution. But a true ring, a
soul lock, and shopping is a delight, what
traces left of tribal pain lessen in the rain
until every necessary transaction brandishes
the rose of time, triumphantly above
the stalls of love. Then the heart and the
mountain range are one. What if the inter-
vening nonsense turned out to be a small
entertainment called City of Fear?


Intervening nonsense called western fear:
anything rather than face the world-
opening it initiated. Dampening, I turn down
a plastic shepherdess at 30p and go back
to the car. And sit there waiting in the rain
for something better than pastoral, some-
thing less fairground and more circus,
something to take the truth of the west-
ern world out of its pocket and purchase
life everlasting or a well meant Friday hug.


No use waiting. Turn the key, go. Go where?
If I went north I'd live in a cold music
for guitar and steelworks and have to face
daily a narrower question over the silver moors,
the treasure chests of bird and slow thought
where the houses cling to the long ridges,
trying to preach like Coleridge that sublimity
isn't simply vertical, but carries grey
rock-juice down into heavenly furrows where
bright minerals sing for dinner, home and away.

Or to speak plainly, pennies are good shit.
If I went west you wouldn't notice me, a
Sunday fisher in the canal, a packed-lunch
gourmet who returns to a brick row with
small back window onto flagged yard and
coke-shed, there to pass the dark hours
in seasonal remembrance. It is a dream
of such fragile substance such unlaundered
currency I daren't speak, the old man in
the shaving mirror, turning the tribal wheel.


Then work is the only credit and it's true but if
I go east the whole scale of action is enhanced,
the great keep rises over the plains, on its surface
reptilian armature twined formally with affection
shield against shield, eye and ear stretched to
soul-pitch across the sky, and all the trim fields
merge into the slow richness of decay. The fewness,
the shifting drone of death, lines a shared crown
on an innocent forehead – patient scholar, mongol
child, and working ploughman, designate the world.


I couldn't go there today, the theatre is hidden
under Restoration scaffolds. I could go south,
to the heart of smooth success, deny the grit of
presence and evade the friction of self-surface
against a viable universe, don't take me there.
Please don't deliver me to that small south, that
smilybox where language oils itself constantly
in inner circles; let me wander still in the open
fields of failure, where the linnet coughs at eve
and the daffydil hides it condom, let me live

longer in the long pain. I won't go south and
enter that gloss. But I did, I went south, why,
for a library, for fear of provinciality, as if that
meant a thing in the corrosive fog of self-
colonisation, because I wanted company.
And come back up here three times a year
for humanity. I'll stay where I am, I'll book
myself back to the bed and breakfast, I'll count
up to fifty and take a deep dinner, followed
by the wine of solitude in the clamouring vale.


So the George again (suddenly it's dark) and
a microwaved lasagne and chips, cheap red
wine a chill draught and a flea-bitten cat
scratching itself at my feet in the otherwise
empty dining-room I couldn't be happier.
I couldn't win a thing on the lottery or
the trials of polity or the small poetry
world, where fleas scratch cats. Goodbye
Cambridge and the 17th century karaoke for
quite a while, I'm bound for the Rio Nègre.


Which is a promise I do keep, in spite of
tiredness and convenience, comfort and cold,
I walk on past the house. The corner wood
moans blue, the former sheep sizzle, I don't
care I walk on past. No hand guides me,
no finger twines with mine, no bleep in the dark
means the Education Department knows where I am.
For once no intelligence in the world has
any knowledge of this route, which is dedicated
against individual gain, to equity as grace.

The path begins to dip then suddenly drops
over the lip, and scrambles down a shingly
waterfurrow right to the base, to the very
reason, and crosses it on a wooden footbridge.
I'm there. So my family of friends, my
squirrels and pigeons shuffling into night
the heron making for roost by the river map
my little hearties my gods and insects
we share a space, and the immensity that
sections me makes for you a set of traps.


How quietly they keep their homes. Told by
the Power, the astrophysics, to seek cover
every night they go. As I beside the river
walk in the kind cold dark an extended
moment thick with arrows. I mean I can't
see the route very well and memory-darts
fill the air: blame, shame, the world's game
I lost before it ever started and wrapped
in failure follow the glint of water, signalling
to my allies that I love their mutual singing.


And in guilty night my ordinary speech asks
after mother, how she lies now, nowhere –
just a pain in my chest. Still complaining,
that language closes the world in tight
darkness and de-recognises souls blazing
with necessity. A little Manchester woman.
And this anger is passed on, with the love,
and gnaws at my oesophagus as I walk blindly
upstream the dry leaves crackle and fall
into dust, a small owl calls into trust.

For trust is the animals' bourne, the very end
of everything they think, their highest music.
Cunning little vixen, fixing your ache in someone
else's cavity who prowls now in the secret vale
moving among trees by the river's edge
like a lost chicken, into whose breast
a sweet message sank and a fine set of teeth
so lovingly you eat me, so quietly the ants tick
in their cells and what a brilliant idea it was,
to die, leaving the answer sung but unspoken.


To lie in bed while someone else wraps
a dark cloak round them and stamps the stony
earth, stumbling on unseen roots and ridges,
always listening for danger. An experienced
city pavement mover, I sense brute resentment
at fifty yards, and routine entrenchment from
shore to shore. O the desperate strains of the
Manchester Sonatas, the barbarity of privilege,
the ruthless violin of fear. A bird's call
crosses that space a few times a year.


And bits of light get down through branches
to the river's shiny upholstery. Long reaches
and very difficult breaks are, with practice,
traversed, walked, passed alongside. I must
be somewhere near the stepping stones under
Cold Eaton and twenty thoughts from company.
A hostelry in my head accommodates this cold night
all the city's homeless and treats them liberally
to cups of Horlicks, warm blankets, dog food,
assurances that society will reconvene shortly.

A hostelry in my head with blocked drains
and a dead duck in the sink. As the homeless
satisfied for a while sleep towards new distress
a diffused moonlight on a frozen windowpane
inscribes a distance that a trust could be
bound to, that a call could come alongside and
enumerate in long song the ancestral victories
one by one; in the wall the small tick of a death
that never dies and all love's cuts be finely
worded, as a dying mallard makes a sentence.


Dying of cold and betrayed by trust as the no-
longer interested company drift away downstream
talking of success in a pub-like ambience.
Leaning into the bank and making a noise,
an understandable noise, that passes through
the dim dark air into the passing passer-by
by the ear, and lodges close to the heart,
joining the company there, of homeless singers
on a train through the night across Poland
to unthought-of terminals, kissing the wire.


Then out of cover into Wolfscote Dale in
dazzling brightness a full moon riding
the crystal scattered sky and the great V
tunnelled before me gleaming, cold, empty,
shining unto itself against the black, deep
star-clear firmament, this whole earth-mass
holding the celestial fact in its arms
quietly and passionately by the white flowers
in the hillside grass holding the sex of a god
in gently murmuring river dale against harm.

And loud and long the constant fall
and strike of water on itself fills the air
on all sides with a continual sounding.
A river works through the night anywhere
on earth as a voice meaning a clear thing,
meaning unspecifically, that earth life
passes, thus and so and that and therefore
admit, that gratitude falls into empty space.
An educated meaning directs work where it is
wanted, and the long tones sing themselves.


Straight and proud, song and singer hand
in hand saying Grant us peace, time and space
fit for thought, again and again at day's
decline levering the voice into the sphere:
nations have mercy, give us a chance. I pray
for the future of the Ba-Benzélé pygmies
of equatorial Africa what else can I do?
but set the soul-light where it comes first
and walk up the moon-flooded dale at midnight
singing waley waley love is unjust.


And they just sat in rows on two tree-trunks
and sang (this was the Aka, in another film or
record) a kind of polyphonic hoquetting that
ran through night and day a total signal of
readiness and comprehension, of liberty and
they did it because 'this is what we do now'.
Also negotiating with distance, that under
these terms we take and return. Think of being
where people are tired of gain, and bored
with advantage and want to hunt down peace.

To a long valley cut through limestone strata
like a gap in a crown, where peace may emerge
brighter in moonlight than the recorded day, on
up. On and on and very gradually up. Biggin Dale
branches off to the right, the whole of history
is in danger of being forgotten. This walk
is a night walk of the world where horizons
meet. In the trumpeting of water a triumph
is sounded for the despised, who meticulously
follow their equitable ways down the dumps.


Like walking a long corridor in a hospital
the bushes in their white coats and this
shiny conveyor belt running alongside bearing
weathering solutions, enzymes, floods of tears
back to the town. Things that reach across.
Plodding on stony track next the stream I
think of teenage lovers, Alzheimer's patients
moving to the world's edge and bearing its content.
The joining of souls is worth all the moonlight
down which eyes draw their long content.


On up, as the fall fits behind, a whole life.
Everyone has a whole life, what happened to it?
What was its final shape? I strain to hear,
above the stream, the grasses in their converse
and over the grasses the silence of air, that
silently stings memory. Failure is meant only
as a way of reaching clarity, its questions, a
life homing in the small hours, what became
of it? Did pride and guilt get it in the end,
did its fire add to the cold? Who or what

Asks this? I look up to the valley rim, dark
against the sky. Bumps on the stone walls
that follow the lip: gods and goddesses,
strolling the fields waiting for dawn,
mandarins and courtesans, arms in sleeves,
pensively avoiding the seated sheep and
stepping indulgently over their dung, thinking
together of ways to mend the world, if only.
For everyone or not at all, in common tongue.
And gather up its history, and sing the long song.


They peer over the stone walls that follow
the valley edges and see me: look at him,
down there, walking the river path up Wolfscote.
What's he doing there? What for? They can't
even tend themselves, those people. They
can't tender the faintest answer, they work
separately. I look down. The river glances
past my side, about four metres wide here.
And still the long tones succeed each other
like penitential bells, exactly on the hour.


As long vales attract extended thoughts,
from the sky or the god fields of reward.
Above the valley the fields proliferate, white
walls round them with occasional stone barns,
double fruit trees and Quaker burial grounds.
Ghostly sages walk there at night, looking
for lost tumuli, for the world-good of every
remotest soul. Down here the creatures of death
forget themselves in rapid displacement and
a sweet harmony pierces the resulting distress

Like an ulcer piercing a stomach wall,
all the stones of the body tossed in acid
align themselves to that sweet singing.
A good thought is itself a sweet song to
which the river is *basso continuo* though
my own speciality is *scordatura*: adding to the
difficulty a lateral shift thus tempting
a world register. Or the final knowledges so
tenuous and watery, *rilievo schiaccito*,
the wound a calm thing, with far to go.


As a wound lived with does become calm, all the
herbs of the valley gather round it saying
Breathe slower, there are other worlds. The lamb
agrees, and dies into distant sandwiches. Ah!
to die in earnest and forfeit your name to a
continuum of credit transactions, it is a sad time.
But forgiven while the flower fairies gather
round the well head singing (sweet) a lament
in long notes, a song partly unhuman, that
trembles through the entire economy torn apart.


Is it not so, rows of dark heads on high
walls, that I walk under, don't the days'
edges wrap the ruins in simple clothes?
And they go back to their perambulations
their night circuits on the upper pastures
humming over fragments of old folk-songs
to themselves in the search for good polity.
The valley continues, lurching this way and that,
a few clumps of trees in the river haze and stripes
of scree on the long slopes, let me go.

Let go of me and I'll give you an answer
if I have an answer to give that doesn't add
to the world's cold. The towns over the hills
are full of ills and answers but the works die
and crumble, the chimney stands at the valley head
derelict, a tower to lost patience. Not this valley,
which never suffered profit, though a negative light
inhabits it now, bearing modernity's favourite message:
No parking. Move on, keep going. No hermitage here,
no respite either. Days and hearts are torn asunder.


Well at least you don't have to pay to walk here,
though I expect the day will come. And yet the days
to come hold no terror but the world's own, how
to work kindness across the gap between one and
many in the light of the fading eye. O for a craft of
wholeness dictating every detail, finish, grace-note,
surety woven across the night and curving straight
into day, shadow's edge doubled in travertine.
Refusing collectivising aids. The delicate brushwork
of the soul courtiers proposes a republic.


Eye-bright, the inscribed line, the river's margin.
And a glow-worm at the path's edge, I thought
it was the world shining in love's desert.
I passed it by in the warm night thinking of
a republic of the (heart, mind) republic of the,
for and by the, soul-light or nothing, top
legal fact. Sitting on the marble bench
outside the Palazzo del Capitano dei Populi
I thought this proudly, and stuttered it
into the punctuated blaze on all sides.

Great pattern of healing… Though time
destroy the person, the intent shall range
the upper levels while mortals sleep, and
patiently, patiently, think-tread the fields,
coaxing lasting peace formulae out of bitter grass.
The stone barns up there get up and move
somewhere else in the night, I have photo-
graphs to prove it. The locals don't notice,
they have television. I said this repeatedly
and cursed the comforting guns but alas,


The box I stood on was of cardboard and pain
became my teddy-bear. I hold it in the night
in bed or a long valley while world routes
traverse the sky. We whisper to each other:
Remember, I was your valley, you walked me
and the black river slid past us, taking
all our vows into storage but we walked on,
keep my hard head always against yours
and our hearts will collaborate in long tones
through vast Europes of burning bones.


Pain whispers through people, and tells them
the truth perhaps walking steadily up the long
winding river dale at night. Poetry occupies its
moment completely, like heroin, it is deeply
convincing, but does it know the truth? Europe
is building a wall against Africa's groans. And you
are a stupid walker who should have been in bed
two hours ago, the world is not listening
to your solitary fantasys. The hospital you failed
to heal in stands at the north end of your head.

Favour at least, is a constant. It finds its way out
through a concealed life, transpires from the
fullest fear: here death has trampled death
and the dippers, so busy in the daytime, sleep
now under the bank in pockets of faint warmth,
as shall I tomorrow, the other side of fearful
thought. Like a hand against a feathered side
faintly warm under a cold bank and ruffling in
electric spasms of dream, I hope to win
an intellectual conviction, O faithless one.


Approaching now a boundary, edge of a reef,
where the sides descend and spread out, and
the god patches round Alstonefield recede into
cloud-land, silver hounds that serve their own
excellence. They get on with our best thought
while the working organism walks the twisty track
racked with fear and anxiety. My toy, my dump, walk
behind me and grip my shoulders in the dark. Under
the rock shelves of an edge nerve, sleeping birds
and victims of nationalism decorate the route.


Resentment rages though the black air surrounded
by transparent calm. Waves of limestone dive
into the ground and great shoals rear up
glowing pale in the night uncertainty and
riddled with caves, in one of which 'A cobbler
his wife and seven children lived within living
memory'. Wattle awnings over the entrance and
in the evenings they sat round a fire singing
a narrative polyphony in divided head-tones
while the weather suited itself and death hung

Suspended. At this junction the river takes
a slight waterfall under a footbridge and vapours
mingle in the air, wrapping night in the flavour
of mortality. It flickers beside the dark land,
poor waterlogged stuff owned as I recall by two
brothers in a stone fortress-farm on the edge
of the dark hill living without hope of marriage
though a cobbler owning nothing but a certain
cultivation, constructed a fortress here against fright
where mutual favour folds the future into life.


Like a wine, like a careful Merlot folding youth
and age the night tolerates the loss of names, yours
and mine, already falling under the footbridge
out of meaning, a junction the other side of which
hope is entire. The river bends to the west and
the cliffs to the east, forming this oval meadow
in which, you remember, the fox dances
with the hare and the lamb adores its tomb;
a swollen space, mandorla in middle night,
full of river mist to chest height.


Nameless we wade in it, a Roman bath, arms
out on the conceptual surface. Histories
float past and we hum their tunes, the little
circles proving one equals zero at the highest
tone. Of what happens we know next to nothing,
but we sway in the vale, take our partners
and run a business without profit from which
a concerned eavesdropper may learn the
tariff of careless love. Relax the throat,
hold harm at arm's length and dance with it.

Round and round as night and star face
each other in the oval purpose in a
clearing of the preoccupied river, that
hurries on by. O I believe, I do believe
that I go back home. I don't think I'd ever
have started this night-long trudge if I
didn't know for sure: I end at the precise
beginning of what I am, the shared declaration.
Catch equilibria out of anonymous tunes
and believe it, the whole mist of speech.


I'm sorry I missed your speech but the rabbit
danced with me in the darkened cove and I
couldn't let his/her shoulder go we were
chest level in the seas of sleep and the air
hung curtains on our eyes. But I remembered
as I foxtrotted around that quasi-circular
pasture something in my origins that Engels
failed to notice in the back streets of inner
Manchester where various things added together
made a hope so long so real and so angelic


We waited a life for it, we got engaged
and in spite of everything raised a shout
of joy, totally disadvantaged we caught
each other at turning-point where delight
transcends critique, declared ourselves
fully and sang our way home in the great
omnibus of the rain. We dance on, the band
shows no signs of fatigue, the floor
is hidden under five foot of fog and me and
my furry friend we flourish at death's door.

I'd like to say that again. There were
angels in the cellar that Engels never
noticed and the government inspector was
one of them. He drank with us and the night
became longer than the alienists could ever
believe or tolerate. The state in fact listened,
understood, and acted; only the aristos,
and the artists, turned up their four noses.
Am I not a plain speaking man, furry friend?
Whirl me to the end, gag me with roses.


Look, this is a serious poem why am I
waltzing with a mammal? Bright his (her)
long teeth shine in the moonlight as we
gyrate across the mead, strong her (his)
clasp behind my neck where ghosts make
their love. The land curves round us in this
abandoned place where people have always
been content to be deprived, turning and
smiling in the face of profit, dancing
the night away and no more, stopping dead.


For the masters of the earth declared (a)
there is no destination for souls (b) we'll
take all the cash thanks. So the rest of us
die quickly, to keep the machine well fed.
To this tune I dance in neck-high mist with
an earth creature at midnight. Bedridden
anxiety in the river's endless loop, red
couplets in the cave mouth squaring the ring
that nations may look at the clocks in the sky
and concentrate on creating liberal space instead.

Shared space, how we danced. Then nothing.
Just water falling over stones in the darkness.
Children left home, pets died one by one,
a voice left grating in the night, digging
in against all this dispersal, advancing in
pitch dark to the end of the meadow where
trees gather and the dale entrance opens
ahead like a hall, almost roofed. Not a
serious route since the Bronze Age. Millions
of lives simple darkness and earth noise.


A far distant voice left, on an old recording
repeating formulae in a fog of surface noise
ain't got no moma now In cielo cerco il tuo
felice volto divining the way to the footbridge
in the dark by memory, by hurt. The earth gives
gently under each step like an abandoned mattress.
Locating direction by wound echo, river noise,
leaf movement, residue. Import floats off behind
up to the god terraces and harvests of cloud.
Guiding myself correctly by ordered words.


Smiling, for nothing else knows how. The trees,
ever restless, cast doubt on walking creatures
who smile. I stop in the middle of the footbridge,
under me the dark river slops on and I look
back down along the curved space as if
I thought maybe a red glowing point in the
pale rock towers at the far end, and over
to the right a couple of street lamps where I
know there are no streets. But men who can't
sleep and have stopped trying for ever.

A fire in a distant cave, brilliant embers
for the end of a life radiating energy not
faint not lost. She was something of a dragon
but she never promoted fear and gloom
for elective gain. So she inherits the grace
of the unpowered and the underpaid, may she
enter nonsense with no more than a good push.
And over to the right, twin lights. All that
work, all that balancing and thrust, what's
left of it but self hatred and failed trust?


What's left of anything is precisely nothing,
trees soil and stones queuing to vanish.
A red light means hope and departure: took
my suitcase to the station and the train went
without me, an ordinary cave receding. So
the old lady converts to nothing in the small hours
and the rest of us continue like street lamps or
endoscopes in the bowel of day, restlessly,
hoping to find for good or ill. And eventually
even the brightest star burns back to nil.


Red flicker where things leave us, white blades
where they advance. Out across the oval meadow
these contraries twine to the music, supplied by
strangers: gypsy on the road fiddle in sack over
shoulder water falling over stones, on his way
to help an old widow die a glowing death, a death
to be proud of a death studied many years ahead
making a red punctuation in the cursive night.
Russet songbirds sleeping under the sod I
lean on a rail over the drainage of fear and loss.

And look at the twin stars under the hill,
the two lights from the bleak farm. In those
corridors there is no death and so no joy
or sorrow. There is aim: work and structure,
masking despair. Difficulty and anxiety confirm self.
It is a long night and the electricity costs more
all the time, owls keep their estate in the trees back
of the dung heaps in brilliant irony while
the moon gets little chance before the hill crest
wipes it. These people burrow into time


And vanish into their shadows. The meadow dance
was a rare moment but what happens is water
falls over stones in the darkness and all the
kindness intimated by formality remains
dependant on a world question: a great deal
more than human if it is to return ever.
So that's the picture, and the night continues
in a murmuring of many voices from many throats
a motherly continuum in the solitary vale
saying wait for me and I'll come back some day.


I'll come back and we shall be reunited, people
who meant something and were lost and died, whose
lives made a writing and now nobody knows where
the writing is. Can I truly read it in the fall of
water over dark stones, the humanless contours of
an earth junction? Phil Davenport was one, musician
from Derby who went to Mozambique and never came back.
A few ill-recorded tapes. Wind and nests in high trees.
An old aunt who viewed me with suspicion as if the world
might not be telling the truth. I was young. Nightjars.

I could have been wrong, but I thought for a moment
over to the right in the wet fields was either a
badly oiled sewing-machine or a nightjar. Probably
not a nightjar. It is very good to be hanging around
in the middle of the night doing nothing but lean
on a rail over falling water, it shows a person un-
curfewed, a citizen not a subject, taking a certain
pride in plural space without disdain. I want to know
who's sitting sewing in the middle of the night,
in dark clumps of reed, joining what and who?


Is it the woman Elaine Scarry speaks of,
whose soul tenderly feeds the future an
improved coat and dies unthanked? Is there then
a selfless self over there in the darkness a
harmless human? The weaver on the moor spins
a solitary thread in ever thickening night,
humming the tune to the tread, a history
of obscure suffering and unrewarded pains
to which the night bird's moan is finely
tuned O Delvig, Delvig, what do we ever gain?


Pure purpose continues upstream to its point
of rest but I leave the river here, sensing a familiar
call, off the footbridge round the tree and onto
the road at the ford O Delvig, what do we become?
Nothing, a great city of it, built up from
a night point. And rain starts, that rain
of which Du Fu speaks, that 'steals through
the night on the breeze, noiselessly wetting
everything'. Rexroth's words. Silently screening
a truth that calibrates the earth.

I join the road running up from the river and
creep along the wall. Carefully, because there is
an electronic device here, on a gatepost, with
a light that questions the night and a button
which if I press either a lump of acid rock
blasts me out of here or the police station
at Leek is alerted. I wish it summonsed some-
thing fairer: a good wine merchant, the poetry
help line, meals on wheels, the monastery porter
(routine kindness in a hurry)'s assistant.


I step out of the small flood plain and walk on
country road at night by pattering trees.
The oval meadow spreads out below me, open
to the sky like real space like a Piazza del Popolo
in which meetings are real and you sit there
sipping the cappuccino while tides of hope
waft the end onwards, air currents that stir
the land, the children leaving school at three. They
play at young foxes and there's both time and need
for democracy before the whole song plunges into the sea.


No strength without purpose. Meetings are real
when just, tonight just me and the night
creatures, the badger shuffling where he must
and little owls among the leaves waiting for dawn.
They occupy their pauses above and below me
as walking slowly I posit a perilous space
called Here we succeed. Indeed I too have sat
sipping stimulants in stone towns, Gubbio, and Todi,
and I know as well as anyone how fully precarious
is hope, the singing in the empty grave.

That whirring in the fields again, like
the jack-snipes in Donegal filling the thick
night air with messages across a vast grey
grave and it seemed at once that all the big
fast transport was flung into the sea, the slow
won every race and the patient established peace
across a republic of mitigated pain. Moving
slowly up towards the crossroads at night a sense
of Reverdy tells me this long asking is short
of answer, at which the night birds wince again.


Halfway up the slope I have a glimpse of
energised stability. It's a road, it's just
a road somewhere in the country, priests
of fear and loathing flit in the dark fields
among silent rain. It's an empty road
and the lights fall far behind, the whole hope
of Italian republicanism lies on the hills
in the form of what we are, an argument kept
alive by interjection of honesty and pride,
my love and I dancing it on the full tide.


Such stillness at the turn. White sound in
black night: thin, swirling rain, brushing and
laving the restless leaves; holding the lost form
of what we are: a struggle, from which a crystal
is gained, something you can see variously
through. A public space, a meeting-place
of conflicting hearts on limestone paving, all
the apertures in the palace facade carved with
intricate sea fauna and symmetrical fruit processes:
good is where it is forced to be, and to excess.

Conflicting purposes run together by force
of wish, working for sectional interests in an
advancing light that casts hope as a reflection,
flicker of flame on the tympanum, yellow webs
swirling on the stone above the fountain. Isn't
history such a finely forced affair? The rain
has stopped, a cloud gap opens and the moon spreads
a paste, a cream cheese of light on all the dim
rural forms that greyly glow in the fields like
a communal purpose in the missals of insight.


And who's this then? Thick rectangular lenses,
white sickly face that catches the moon and
throws it back. Hardly any lips at all, just a
wobbly line of mouth turned down at the ends,
wisps of hair on a permanent preoccupied frown –
who's this coming down the road with a stick,
what's this ghost in a horrible check sports-
jacket far too wide on the shoulders? Dmitri!
I shout, is it you? I suffer, he whispers,
from the most abominable indigestion


And cannot sleep. Why is he wearing glasses in
the night anyway? Why isn't he tucked up in bed
or buried in his fear twenty years ago? Energised
stability, how did you escape? I suffer, he says,
from people's abominable imaginations whereas
everyone knows the world is an unalterable sum,
of which we and everything we see are temporal
processes, to the strains of unlimited tangos.
Party officials float overhead howling in pain,
declaring a new age again and again and again and again.

A bowl of pain in small night. A light burning
across trackless fields, a production unit
that doesn't know how to stop. Prison farms,
concealed zones in the traffic arrangements, acrid
smoke that no one can bear to notice, drifting
across the plains. And why, I ask him this, why,
I grab hold of his shoulders, we've known each
other a long time, I don't shake him, we stand
face to face on the dark road, there's some
trace of bodily substance under the padding, I want

To know what all that was for, I don't shout,
I don't speak, he knows what I mean, where is
the finality that resolves the loss? He doesn't
answer, but the thin lips curl into a lost smile
and there's a sound in the air of his head like
what you get if you wind something up, a relentless
ticking music, as empty as the edible nothing all
round us; ghost sonata, mindless banality, a yes
from which the heart has been removed. Shallow,
O Shallow Brown, you're going to leave me.

I was interested precisely in staying put, I didn't want
to rend or bend or pump up anyone's heart, I never
traded in disappointment; the only departure I know
is of everything: Italian socialism, art, mossy stones,
wedding dances and country games on the green
it all gets sucked into the chimneys of the
meat farm leaving nothing but a space: no record
survives, no marketable loss. And this is why
I hiss and rattle in the night, and on this last
and lonely night declare finally that love is

Nothing. Love raised the death camps. The ticking
fades, trust flies up to the hill tops beyond
the fields and resides there in prenatal grandeur.
No thank is paid; we reside on the earth we eat
and breathe it, and sing back a cold lament under
the moon, a dispassionate exercise in fidelity.
Earth's future, the whole physics, the possible
routes across it, the whole chiming circling concept
places a stiff finger on the back of my neck and
propels me up the dark road, coughing in tune.


Musician, be different. For God's sake stop
singing and tell me something! Shallow Brown,
don't e'er deceive me. It's very late: love
took its due years ago and scattered us
across the world shouldering affection like
a knapsack. I hold his shoulders, and on
the narrow road beside the long wood we are
face to face with silence. Let me fail, he says,
musically. Luchistaya zvezda, chim ozaryon
syanyem kray, mne danny dlya rozhdenya.


Radiant star, whose light sheds its light
on my poor origins, only from you is there any
reward. Love withers in the desperate beams, the
desperate simplicity of service, doing exactly
what is asked of you. How do you find it, then,
Dmitri, here in the so-called liberal states,
treading the graves of gypsy musicians not an echo
in the night – what's the tune in that case alive *with*?
He never turned and never answered and was
not there, croaking untransmittable wrath.

It was terrible, there was a sick man hobbling
down the black road then there wasn't. Either
of these would have been hell. Do you think
politics explains these apparitions, do you think
adjustments at the top will change everything?
Don't you think death was all along the only
adversary and ever is? Talk yourself out of it,
pass round the red tartlets, tomorrow is my
wedding day, brown is my silky hair, where
did he go? What's the pain of an average tree?


Is in its heart, used for waste paper. I try to
call him back: Dmitri! I shout into the road-
side bushes above Barrack Farm but there's
nothing, he's gone down to the black river
behind my back and the fields shroud over again
as the moon turns in. The experts were all wrong:
musician-poets, loss merchants, marketeers of
graveyard tablets saying Long he loved and
longer died, step aside, corporate pride, here
comes Pity. The blazes with pity. 'We don't want


Charity we want justice.' I carry my thought-radio
on my back, aerial aloft. It tells me to walk on
through such certainty. Boletus flourish at
certain times of year in the wood over to the left.
I remember this from when I lived here. That move
into the entire land when a couple becomes
a family, that optimism, took place in the big
stone house over there. There I leant on the wall
at summer's end far from any metropolis, and counted
the faithful on one hand, the successful on another.

For the world can go one way or the other.
There is a choice, of emotions, up or downhill,
there is a music that emphasises loss, and
another, tense with patience, quis dabit
pacem populo timenti. Listen to it, spell
its every move in the night, wherever you
are, daughter, brightness beyond the shadow's
edge, far from home, queen of the becoming
machine. O daughter, the green meadows that
lie between us, flecked with white bone.


So it is to reach the watershed crossroads
and be newly old. Across every field and
acreage of pasture is a life subscribed to
by will or nil, attached for ever. Loss
is then an intention, exactly conceived
and perfectly delivered, the true outcome
of desire. This was she to me and knew it,
and knowing departed, full of fear. In
that stone house, quietened now by night,
the progressive meadows opened from a point.


A point of contact. How should I know what
happens in the world? To know is an evasion.
This walk at its furthest point relinquishes
the driver's seat and stands nowhere at the dark
junction not knowing which direction to take
or what shall ever be the gain. But remembering
gladly the fires that burned in that stone house
over there many years ago and sadly the way
time rolls us onward, trouble in mind. Hell-
hound at the crossroads, pulling everywhere.

The coal-fires burning with the bright snow outside
and the eastern wind. The clocks, the radio news,
the baby on the floor and safety established in
all the land. Hound, be a worthy dog, and faithful
to my side. Trot beside me through the long
night, fetching images at request. Ticking
banality, delay your despairing. Earth forces
surrounded the house beating the slated roof
with bats of forgetful air. None of it means
anything but a long track from a death to a birth.


The brightness means wholeness, the darkness
means look harder: wholeness too. Tall,
snowy beauty, year after year to look out
and see the time returned, the horse chestnut
tossing and the flakes borne up on the wind.
And in this doorway she and she returned.
And in this closure you and I survived. In
these passing violins the future of Europe
suffers a small aperture of hope, that
glows redly through the nightly smoke.


Glows pale across the fields, central affection.
Maps hoisted above the hedges, but it doesn't
matter, where to go. Don't ask, 'Where am I going?'
Ask, 'Where does such tenderness come from?'
– right there within the arms' arc, a point
that generated a history, a nothing that ran
right round the clock and back to itself year
after year as the moment fruited the bees
took their reward and the child that bright
instant spoke out a new justice. Where is she now?

Where fear propels and forks the path, or delight
opens into space. I'm starting to fade. Joy
lies like a stone on the ground. Pick it up.
'I am alone in the night, a homeless and
sleepless nun, holding the keys to the city',
and talk it onwards, wherever you are. Carry
also something for the passing stranger.
Such are the demands of equity as love sinks
across the dark hills with the rain. I am
absolutely nothing in the showered grain.


The showered grain, the shadowed gain.
Complete silence at the crossroads, the white
railings and the sombre fields between the
dozy roads. North south east and west
where's the one I like the best because best
known, and get the knowing back. I drape
myself on the railings, towards a sleeping
lamb in a wooden crate. Daughter, let me be
a shadow on your fear, a weight on your
ambition, a red glow in your hate.


Let me think. Directions available are again four.
I could slide uphill south where leisure rules. If
you're tired go to bed and let the world find itself.
I could return to east and live in a document
of what wasn't except as what survives. I could
turn to north without hope of anything but
achievement. I could continue, west, downhill,
and a lot of trouble in uncertain devolutions
of the heartland curving back in. Whatever I decide
there is somebody watching me across a field.

Across every field there's someone: loved, lost,
asleep in the big house or standing there at
the far corner in a white dress, world bride,
holding a small bouquet, looking this way.
Suddenly breaks into a run and dashes along the
field wall to the left, a pale moving blur that
crosses the path I haven't yet decided to take,
over the road and into the tin chapel. I heard
the door slam, the dim light appear in the broken
window, the old harmonium lurch into All For Thee.


Such tenderness dive-bombs despair. She gets
married in the tin chapel beside the road. At this
point I bow to gravity and move off to westward,
the downhill contract into continuance. Walk
beside me on the heavy grit while the June
flower heads nod us away; I'll walk out with you
any day, O faithless one. And merrily I do, down
a starlit road, between fields where cares rest,
and past a tin chapel or meeting room
in which my daughter gets married, perhaps


I wasn't invited. Perhaps I was and forgot.
I won't disturb them now, I'll pass by.
Out through this curved horizon is an open
hope to which their promises are acrobats.
Archford Moor, ridgeback sandstone inlier
topped with poor farmland, fields of pasture
broken by small patches of marsh grass.
A lame man and his Polish mother inhabited,
as I recall, the one farm. Their promises
are a bridge to the world's long strings.

The dim light in the tin shack, two or three
witnesses, gently spoken words projecting
an optimism in which the landscape is cast
under and there is a crack or error in our
persistent elevation of the world that
time's cynicism can't fill; the moment it
lives in sweeps through the trees as their
promises take my hand and sing me to my
journey's purpose. In solemn agreement
to maintain each other, a sense of flying.


Steadily down past the chapel, cracked windows
glowing fore and aft like high windows in a
vast city as the pedestrian walks beneath, where
a healing is taking place, or preparation for
a birth. To pass so close to it, those silent
acts carefully memorised, belief unstated in
duties clearer than any verse, putting the singular
in direct contact with the totality. Why other-
wise bother? Writing books, learning a trade,
rolling in cloudy certainty down long straight roads.


Deep in the small hours (persisting through
the dark doors, trusting to the end) anthems
receding in the night as I walk on down the
long road glowing faintly in starshine and
the black overshadowing trees humming aloud
to the old refrain: If you love the world
follow its instructions. And gain an advocate,
even the spirit of truth (in the original orth-
ography 'sprit'). Mulling this over again
I didn't notice I'd entered a domain.

'Explain yourself,' said the landowner, last time
I was caught in this wood, which was nearly twenty
years ago, idling around admiring the blooms
of fly agaric when the person, the person entitled,
appeared askance, and explained that it was private:
private woods, private toadstools, private elves
sitting on them knitting, the whole scene as private
as a child-rape. He returns in this dark underleaf
and stakes his demand: What are you doing here? Ex-
plain yourself: 'Love raised the death camps.'


Indeed, they meant well, the ventured words,
determined lovers all, they all meant well
but they raised death camps and it might have been
better if they had stayed unloving and without purpose,
if they had got on with an honest trade and not
plunged to a world focus on the wings of negated
despair. My words are barely concealed thrones
for myself, my rights are insubstantial; I shall
do as the person says and return to the recently
privatised public highway in decentred submission.


My words are unconcealed thrones for my loves
right down the road, right down the right
of way long and straight it goes between
fields and woods like a night-mail express
bringing an urgent question: Loving exactly
what? is the question. And all or nothing
is an easy answer, a word or two. Love knows
no parameters, responds to no need, serves no
purpose but its own and refuses all languages.
*Them people up in th'ills, them's dirty and stupid.*

Who said that? Nothing near me but stone and
fibre, trees gathering over me as I get down
towards the river. What kind of love delivers
such messages? Some kind, certainly, some loving
home with its family values that mustn't
spend beyond its means. So keeps tight like
a pine cone in the night – daughter, forbear the love
if necessary, time like a rolling dream takes most
of it away. Leaving you cold but bound in honour
to the distant tribes who sleep in the far hills


With no advocation but the spit of truth. Left
at the junction, uphill and first right past
the doctor's house (sleeping but on-call) then
steeper down, turning through the middle of the
old mill. The little stall they put out here,
of potted herbs and lusty perennials, stands
roadside in the night. I am seriously tempted
to take one. Both to pay for it and not to,
are a temptation. But this isn't life, this is
love and war. I pay and don't take one.


50p lighter in pocket, awake and on-call but
no one ever calls, down towards the river bend
I hear the sound of it again, the soft beating
manifold tumbling of water on its course getting
gradually nearer like entering a city. Again into
edge zones, and reef miseries, again into
lowland broth. The river bass thumps it out as
the road skirts the river bend past a silent cottage
and a side road where there's a public telephone box,
which starts ringing as I approach.

About 1 a.m. River bass humming alongside,
miles from advancement or delay on a small road
in a geology of violent disruption happening
very slowly over vast stretches of time, like
the dream of a nationless economy (Italian, say,
or sub-Saharan) beginning slowly to assert itself
across the northern plains where the worker at
day's end sits in real time. All the questions I ask
pass unanswered behind my persistent foot-
work when suddenly a phone box rings.


'Explain yourself,' half a voice says. I'm sorry:
wrong words, failed nations like old soup, they
meant well but congealed in the cold world's fear.
Ironical clicks to this, and an electronic drone,
a channel adrift. Then a kind of purr which means
you're on your own, mate. But I am never alone.
Look here, it says, that demi voice, those people up
there in the villages, are foul and mean. All I can say
to this is that the only trustable percepts are of
detail and whole. Hug me Mr Mole, I'm home!


*Oh I'm so glad to see you, sit down in front*
*of the fire while I put the kettle on. Where*
*have you been all this time? I was worried,*
*I was…* and he sorts the cocoa and drops
a match into the ring, the dear old fellow
with his heart in a sling: Old Mole, hesitant and
polite, connoisseur of sheltering arcs. Gently
in the cosy grave behind the waterfall he
offers his slippers to a total stranger and
hums lamentations into the azimuth of war.

I drifted into a certainty, a hole in the sands
of my head dug by middle-class children on holiday
led to a night shelter at the base of knowledge. There,
small-scale conformist anxiety sprouted a belief:
virtue is what people return to. Virtue is original.
Soldier Mole closes the circle and intones the office:
*Here's your cocoa, are you comfortable, let me put*
*this shawl round your shoulders and I'll sit down*
*here to the side. I'm so happy that you're back,*
*I really am. The world is a hateful place.*


In a rock shelter in my night mind a retired worker
mixes a bittersweet cup and encourages further
warmth from a glowing log by poking it with steel.
Sparks rusticate the night sky. Full knowledge
is surely love's bible and the people are the lexicon.
I go this way and that, straight and crooked, my
daughter passes across the sky in a Chagall copula
and the artisans of Zaïre set up a whole-night rhythm
screaming for peace. But nothing unites the im-
possible choices. We solve into bits and pieces,


We heal into death. We vote ourselves out of
democracy again and again. The earth offers
suffocation. The tumbling water echoes in the great
cave-shaft by Apes Tor, water folded over water,
falling beneath water to the underground wheels
pulling water back from its earth. Is this a music
to dance to? Or to sing true and complex, like Seán
'ac Dhonncha in his old tweed jacket, floreation on the
walls of the ancestral cave, singing fate into a caul,
with tales of industry and long slow fall.

In a night glimmer in a slowly descending syllable
I heard an elderly gentleman welcome me to
his humble house and offer me the earth.
I settled the headset back on its rest for an end
to questions, I pushed open the door and
re-entered slow thought, dark road, happy
to shed a tear for the unquestioning souls
of cosy moles, now coasting homeless in the
fell mists. May the adventures they renounced
leave them wise to the world's twists.


For really, the smallest scale of kindness
steps out of history and stands on its own
floorboard against corruption. How real is that?
Here I divide into two travellers. One goes left,
up the hill and over Ecton on a hard slog to Wetton Mill.
The other carries on with the road as it is,
reaching the same or similar point on the level,
twisting this way and that as the river valley goes,
letting the question pass. I intend no lessons,
I figure policy by the cramp of my toes.


The slow song unfolds earth's theatre
at a dark scene, of bitter sisters, cruel water on
the shrinking leaf. Then no one way to go: no
success without harm. Now there are two of me,
one each side the great hill, and the hill between us
full of vast winding hollows, immensely deep
pools and falling noises – long abandoned
copper mines, spasmic histories. Each of me
takes the industrial echoes to heart like the last
waltz: Good night to yous all and God bless.

Well we need our anxiety. I follow the river down.
The folding here is spectacular and rightly
text-book. In the night it stands as a thing
of millennia while school parties and solitary
selves pass below with their notebooks and
note in their books, 'This big arch of black
rock made me think that the earth is a thing
merely witnessed by me and all my kind, miss.'
I test the path at night as if I were blind, I release
my free selves to the old world's mind-stress.


Dr Williams, whose house I recently passed, if
he's still there, was a good doctor, he knew
the limits of his science and rested a hand on
a thinning arm. Maybe the war was a good war,
it made us belong, and live to a singular purpose.
Now we live outside that small home for ever or
destroy everything. The world changes but not radically –
it multiplies its answers. Can a dark valley
with a swift stream can a walked value in a
riven dream teach outer solitude to the world team?


Can I teach a fish to swim, or bird to die? I
pass by the old adits along the foot of the
broken-backed hillside. Noises resound within,
of someone striking a match, of icicles falling
onto stone floors. But still I hear that singing
in which everyone joined like a wooden ship moving
out from berth. They sat round a fire in the night
(the Ake again) singing need out of the original
compact for safety while the girls fastened papaw leaves
to their bums and swayed to the absent light.

I wasn't there. I never shall be. I'm some dreadful
concoction of various trading possibilities, I was put
together by church-goers on a Saturday. Tennis courts
on the southern bounds of Manchester were my pre-
natal sunset. They traded happily there, tit for tat
and well within their means. So what went wrong?
And here we are fifty years later haunting the night
of some derelict valley dreaming of a slow sad
Transylvanian music to lull the heart from fear, or
an African rap to wake the soul from sleepy war.


The blind sleep of real war, which is never far away.
Yet a madrigalian sobriety on the other side of the earth
nurses the feather hope, the Ake or was it the Dorze
in their pauses from laceration chorusing the prize,
the netted death. A music to heal the not-yet hurt. I hear it
in the night hush and marching under the copper spire
I notice clearly how it speaks woe to the city
and solace to the single life, with great relief.
Softly under the rustling berries at the river's edge
I stoop: fear and loss become agents of peace.


Which brought the edges of the sky nicely
knotted to the hearth: there was a law at last.
And O the ease with which she sails those top
notes! Saying that death's welcome is not
an individual skill, or self-heart stadium, but
a mutual cognition, a history. The bushes
on the valley sides ejaculating maroon berries will
confirm this to the letter if approached officially.
The law is my passport, and after many years of
shirking trade I walk lighter for a shared skill.

I walk beside an empty hill, its stomach
rumbles to my left. It's like the news, or
what's happening to the world, how it gets more
complex and the language breaks up. Actually
it lies quiet until someone provokes it. I walk
beside a thundering emptiness, a truly enormous
fellside hits the base just here in a scatter of gravel.
Looking up at it I know it ticks within, I know
supply takes most of the energy, I know my right
is fallen through surface, O my son

Absalon, would I had died before the warlords
began to rule the earth and robotise the fair contours
of the human map, our many ways of falling.
At the bridge I turn left, and scrape open the gate
onto the old winding road that hugs the hill's
foot and so avoid a bureaucratic directive which
pushes itself into most corners of the geography.
I'll stick to a narrow track that grants me the width
to accompany my child, still conceptually hung in
the crook of my elbow like berries in the previous May.

In dark night there are always lights, little glimmers
at the edges of vision, sudden streaks by the roadside
when you look again it's black. No one knows
what they are. Perhaps one of the millions of
the dead, had a bit of harmless energy left,
perhaps mineral friction. Or the plain inability
of the human species ever to know exactly
where it is or what goes on – that such a thing
should shine! If only for a moment, an elsewhere
flutters on the verge, and the far stations merge.

I am in favour of that merging, and the dispersal
of claimed centres. Simple gifts delight me, wishes
and distances set in the certitude of recognition,
the song cupboard, reliquary of the self locked
in the world's thusness. At the bridge I turn left
into the quietest section, a mile of the smallest
of roads, just about car-width and riding the
undulating hill-foot through hawthorn thickets
and oak sets where in the daytime small birds
constantly connect, and small hopes collide.


Before me the night's strata recede, occasional
tunnel entrances to the left. How's the other one
getting on over the other side, I wonder, maybe
on the top now? Would he dare to walk up there among
the summit ghosts? Would he unpack a sandwich
in the night courts where only the future stands a chance?
Would he greet his own fear on the bare mountain?
Down here in covert I share thoughts of quiet health
with sleeping birds. Coal tits and nuthatches
dream me through their territories towards light.


The graceful daily furs they wear are the scores
of a constant music. And isn't there again
a distant choral singing in the air? Dead miners
carolling under the hill, Dervishes turning
under blackened domes, evening in Iron Age Africa
where puffs of white smoke from clay smelts
drift across the village to no one's disadvantage
and the ring is struck, the wedding or shopping ring
is sung right round from zero to nought
echoing in delight or the whole fabric breaks.

Charcoal-burners deep in the English forests, high
as kites, singing through the night, turning and
turning in the distinct life, choir-boys dancing in
the side-chapels of Italian cathedrals, under frescoes
by Simone or Cimabue by candlelight, poetical histories.
Carolling hurt. Coming home from hurt and calling
out to a remote tenderness in the deep mountainous
minds and mines of the people in remote clefts between
accidence and malice. 'I asked one of these blacks
where they get these songs, *Dey make 'em sah.*


'How do they make them? after a pause – *I'll
tell you, it's dis way. My master call me up and order me
a hundred lash. My friends see it, and is sorry for me.
When dey come to de praise meeting dat night dey
sing about it. Some's very good singers and know how,
and dey work it in – work it in, you know, till dey
get it right; and dat's de way.'* I think I hear it
in the far marriage shed of this trembling night,
rustling in the woods behind me as I walk on,
silent and alone until I reach a café-bar.


Which would seem unlikely here, disused country road
in the earth's darkness, gates to open and close,
sheep droppings on thin gravel. But there seems
to be a light ahead. No buildings on this stretch not even
a barn pray God someone hasn't set up a hope camp.
No, just a light, that substantiates as I approach
into the hatch of a white caravan, with a person in
cooking clothes leaning on it, waiting for custom.
What would you like? he, or she, asks. Very little
actually, in the obtaining politics, but suggest a cocoa.

A hiss a gurgle and there it is. *I must owe you something for this.* You'd think so, she (or he) says, and nothing else. I sip and get stared and grinned at and hesitate to ask: *I don't suppose you get many customers along here at this time of night do you?* In ten long years, sir, you're the first. But 'many customers' is an ailment I have sought assiduously to avoid. It is better if the night passes itself sleepily under the dome of leaf friction, than vast promises that no one ever believes. Then

Leans over, presses a bony forehead against my temple and whispers in my ear. *The principle is very clear. To construct a space in which worth is realisable and whatever anyone is bears its meaning forward so that the time lived, always at an end, holds at any point its own prize where the transaction is returned across hope. This is simple, is virtue, is the act of the unacknowledged giver.* I know, but my heart shakes for the cold world. I turn my back and listen to the curled river.

The night is full of holes, our lights destroy them. *She nurst him back to life and coverd up her hed, not to be known or seen.* Black holes that maintain us. Love is fragile and deep, I cannot cross it, I cannot know what it will do: she chooses, she is the darling of my heart. So the night's gaps and ditches fasten my collar to its bone and this slave of wholeness brandishes a fork over a plate in thought's morning.

Actually I think a well toasted sausage at
this point would be entirely redemptive. Right
you are guv, she (is it?) says and the whole
sizzling thing gets under way. But what do you
do here in the long night, I ask (thinking: what's
the source of supply?) these ten years past (what's
the subsidy behind this bounty?) *I turn, sir,
in the simple life* (where's the hammer that
halved your heart?) O canny at night, bonny
at morn, where's the victim of your scorn?


The sausage however is in no points lacking.
There is no problem with the sausage. The back
of the caravan seems to recede into the hill
and the small birds keep their distance singing
Lemady O Lemady what a lovely lass thou art
in their sleep, which is safe yet. I ask again
but get a re-run. We sketch a zodiac on the counter
which we never travel, we turn from our quests
into a work-pot. The stars on the edges of rock
formations call time and the trees grow tall.


Thank you and please accept this potted herb. S/he
doesn't hear me, revolving in the kitchen fume to an
old tune like a hilltop heretic in pre-France, soon
to be fumigated right out. Innocence is so
dangerous, and the leaves of the tall trees
fall one by one to the ground. Don't you know,
I think, the danger you put yourself in wanting
only to love and give? No you don't and I
love you for it, but the dark world in fitting suits
blasts you to a caravan called nonentity.

I tread off without farewell. I was never convinced
this person existed. I look back and sure enough
the whole stage set has vanished. O Schubert,
build us tempiettos of our fears we are all very
close to not existing. Long tunnel mouths to
the left like other people's long talking mouths,
in which we recede to zero with the news.
I say it's not history and listen to the dark, listen
to its speaking moment as the dreaming martins
offer themselves to each other on quick wing.


Moon, where are you? There hasn't been a hint
of elucidation since yesterday but a lamplit room
in Cambridge and a slow bottle culling the dark for
fortitude, where are you moon? Busy somewhere else,
watching other grassy slopes, real heroes and villains
hiding in the shadows clutching guns and Bibles… ?
Once when I couldn't sleep, I was about ten, I crept
to the window moved aside the curtain and looked out
onto a plot of suburban gardens transformed, turned
to silver, the sparkling glass of someone's old age.


And my delight was in the theatre of what is
not yet languaged, clearing apart from harm, cryst-
allised night in which kindness sleeps coiled.
There, it seemed, is the real world not yet coded,
not yet reduced to its own goodbyes but lying there
glittering in the night. In that brief space we could
ask the answers, re-set the terms and bear a bright
currency into day the guarantor of truth before
the moon sets and the entire stage of lawns and
rockeries dims and the mind returns to its daily sleep.

So sleep, Bo-peep, walking sleep and talking sleep
dreaming of an electronic pastoral which bypasses
the industrial conurbation saying: This is not history
and this is not a city, a city is a slighter structure
finely engraved at the heart of a commerce a liberal
and rewarding centrality. Not a growth. The tide
of night runs back, the dream of equity streams on
the dark valley-side under the elected star-heads
confirmed at a series of hi-tech fulcra or ganglionic nodes.
So they sing, and die, delicately across the earth.


There is no other lamp to this grinding walk, but
the purple protein and flickers of bombed cities
reflected off the cloud-base as I feel my way
among the boughs of the lonely ash-grove, thinking
of you. At the dormition of my greed the saintly
passerines gather round, ringing in my ears.
'Nothing is certain', they say. I wouldn't dare,
in Cambridge, say such a thing, though it's true.
But I do, and win some time that death won't ever
get back, and clutch it through a shrinking track.


Reaching Wetton Mill on tiptoe because people do
actually live here. And think back thirty-one stanzas to
Apes Tor where Self Two took off to the left. He
has no time to fall with the leaf he is dialectically
driven. He accepts the cocoa and while Old
Mole's in the toilet dreaming of lost seductions
helps himself to the life savings and slopes off
silently in the night, leaving the door open.
I expect to meet him here about now. I expect
to kiss his brow, I don't know how.

Leaving the door ajar I return to the stately night.
And hating all this love take the left lesser and more
demanding road onto higher ground that bears
the great hill towards the vale. I feel ill. But I always
feel ill, I've felt ill for as long as I can remember
night and day and night again and haven't kept
quiet either. Another fond familiarity, another star
on the Christmas tree, to you I describe the aura of
my decay as I would to few others. Schubert, build us
tempiettos of our fears, containing martyred brothers.


It's easy enough at first and I think when this is all
over I shall have two eggs for breakfast. Wrapping
my future in a napkin I go softly under the cottage rows
clinging to the hillside, without waking a dog. The shoes
of this text, recommended for poetical discretion, are
Clarks, with firm soft soles. And the little lake still there,
down to my left, former power to the mine-weirs,
and the fishing lodge at its corner which I once wanted,
knowing I couldn't stay here, wanted that hold,
wanted a corner when everything else was sold.


Wanted it, a roofed room on the corner of a reed-
choked lake, one big window over the water and
a loft you could sleep in though Gods knows
what you'd do for a toilet. Anyway it wasn't for sale.
And I hadn't got any money. I mention it in passing
as I pass it and it passed me in 1973 and we all pass
the world's small and peaceful places with a touch
of despair. Perhaps I could have been happy there.
Perhaps I could have gone out of my mind in screaming solitude
and hypochondriac mania without troubling a soul.

All quiet then on the downland side. But a distant
roaring from the ridge top as the little road zig
zags along its flank creeping gradually higher:
sharp right, straight up, sharp left, on, I don't know
why I put up with it, frankly, this dark and overscaled
topography pulling me over the contours and the trees
what few there are alive in a new wind. The only thing
I know that keeps me to this demand is I suppose I know
it can be met, I know we have made things to equal all
its banging doors. One of them is Fretwork playing Lawes.


I think so, as I recall, I think that would answer
this aggressive night-pitch, this relentlessness.
I've got arthritic fingers, backache, a sliding
hiatus hernia, frontal headache, chronic bronchitis,
periodic nosebleeds, tinnitus or something in my
head that sounds like a tape-looped starling and I
love the whole set-up, the vast biological space-
pitch that holds living in a constant tension of
one death played against another by inaccessible laws,
like Fretwork playing William Lawes, like inflamed tendons


Burning in the limbs to illustrate the earthly form.
This paining by which to earn life I do adore it. I
wouldn't have it any other, I wouldn't pitch a note in
any other scale. I'd paint this procedure as a
cross of heavy strokes, of earth-colours riven with
occulted light, blood traces on a working surface,
pink and orange tones overpainted by an increasingly
violent night. It would stand single as a sign
on a small road, a splash on a wayside stump,
where earlier haters moved to love's strict design.

And move I do: back there I crawled or was carried
between home and office but this is striding country.
Legs, one of the few sections in good working order
impel me up the ridge side, clown on a unicycle my
head spinning with sinusitis or whatever it is (what
is it? Is it me? Or is it it? Is it that dark knocking at
the door again?) O Doctor Doctor you'll have to run
to keep up if you want to conclude this consultation.
I am after all the living image of a god, the winter nights
are coming and my duties not yet done.


My body is a screen of the world's progress.
It hurts, it fights itself, the mind contradicts
itself and the cold sloping stone burns all of it
in a righteous fire. Author of unsent complaints,
to the government, the police, the broadcasters, God,
the nearest businessperson – that's me, burning in a fire
of defiance and fear. A fire in a hole. Then nothing left
but thin sticks of bone in hillside grass, bits of home,
twitching with wanderlust. When the whole takes over,
when I'm driven to earth, remember me if you must.


On this side the hill remains sealed. I don't hear
any singing, no inner space resounds, all I hear
is the foul rush of air. All the fools who died,
soldiers, miners, worked themselves to nothing
for nothing and now sound like nothing ever happened
as the wind sweeps over the ridge from westward
and hisses down the stony fields I turn towards it.
I have to settle this, I take a small stile in the wall
and go straight up the hillside to meet my bride,
gather ye rosebuds someone paid for all this.

I'll tell ye what befell me: Cupid pressed
the rosie niplet of her breast and the cream
of light fell to the dark earth writing walls
and contracts across the fell ground rising and
falling. So these pale daylight markings on
night pages where all the lives involved are passed
into nothing, every living thing. One such
stony sentence leads me straight up the hillside
through a small quarry and onto the top.
On the top is a mine ruin and love-strife.


Knifed ground, I struggle onto it. And try to
stand up but the wind blasts over the top, tears
my hair, pushes the snot back up my nostrils,
I can't stand it; I duck under the wall and fists
to cheeks crouch under the holy border. Then
turn onto my side clutching my legs on stones
among stone mounds and close my eyes as
the force of force tears above me – let it.
Let it howl and win and work us until we're
finished. Then crouch and roll into the great bin.


And die working, die at pitch. I'm saying you can
have me, astrophysics, biology, industry, war, what's
the difference, do what you like with me. And
a faint flute tune carried in my head which if I
go now I'll take with me, a whistle in the night,
a tone-row held in the cracks of my skull. Shrink-
wrapped head to knee I swirl it round my brain
and roll on the barren ground. Damn you,
the silence I contain here and the musics
circulating in it are all I ever found.

Then realise I'm quite peckish and sit up to
unpack an egg sandwich. While quietly munching
this and minding my own business I am aware
of a strange whistle in the night over and
apart from the wind's desperate barrage. And
wonder what it is. A whistling might be expected,
but that it should whistle the final chorus of
Act II of *The Triumph of Time and Truth* is not.
Perhaps it's just a gentle burdock in the barren field,
a numb sentry carolling she knows not what.


But the tune remembers what we forget and carries it
from one life to the next, the Scythian word-processor
in the stone mound wrapped in blue silk, repeating
again and again the story of the beads, the grateful
lining of the trade routes across mountain ranges.
Only a remembering person could move on such tracks,
secured from harm as reward relayed from self to history
burns roadside palings into the night sky. Now also,
to die were sweet and I bend again to my Beaker
posture for the ice of day lodges in my sigh.


The high wind pushes the clouds away and
the fearful stone-heaps on the ridge-top beam
their stasis each to each. I was cruel to both
my parents, I denied their claim to live forward
through your children which was all they had
after the war. Mother in self-pain howling for exit,
father seeking a quiet answer in despair. I'm clenched
knee to forehead rocking like a Russian doll.
About 1953 prosperity and comfort stopped in their haste
and became mental torture of directionless waste.

And I sing as I roll like a Peruvian mummy, *I thought you were true as the stars above.* But the stars bend and break our heads. Something like a dead crow shoots across the sky something like a worker's soul *What have you to show for years of working? Worn-out boots and damaged lungs, children in flight...* Out on the minefields long years of slowly cultivated resistance, a chorale sung under great hills, lessons fixed in the heart through mutual deliberation and confirmed in the couple-dance, geology and flesh, all suddenly nothing.


Slow formation of a structure of substantive rights maintained by discursive education and realised in active solidarity with periodic knees-up. Cancelled overnight, outright, and for ever. 'Behind the times'. *Public good* translates as *business interests* there is a strange sense of déjà-vu as we creep home, and the economy is saved, hoorah. But the economy is not what we live, the economy is our enemy, casting us into a future of empty tombs, grey prairies scattered with Disneylands eating their own


Flesh for lunch as if a market could be its own motor and spin itself to the top privilege without someone somewhere footing the entire account. We refuse to die into this economy. The songs carried in slow centuries bear purpose larger and more singular than state, and turn the benefits back to earth offering an escape route to central distances where despair and love build cairns on the horizon and passion lights bonfires in hollows of bankrupt night. Throw the book into the sea, the balance, and applaud the metropolis crumbling into its own goal.

I might have said something. The sky blasts the ridge-
top cairns, throwing every fertile particle into the vale,
a deathly movement of air protects us from the
stars we see distorted through its tide and crouched
under the nearest leeside arbour I moan into my ankles
and await the interlocutor I know is expected, indeed
invoked. I wince and cower and offer for the third
time to roll into history and be forgotten. My stomach
twists itself sideways in the philosophical onslaught
of ultimatum and shooting pains herald Urizen.


But no one comes. My left temple twitches,
finger-lock on ankles burns, can't hold this
foetal position any longer. Release myself into
relaxation exercise 24: breathing very slowly
out as the shoulder muscles unclench. Will
this prolong my life at least past four o'clock?
Down by the docks I bid my love farewell
as the slow boat moved out like a piano study
in triple arpeggios *don't you e'er deceive me*
and eventually return. If you will, if you dare.


But no one returns, no one turns up, up on
the godless terraces there's nothing but a raving
wind and dark ground with pale stone forms tracing
the night's vacancy. I anticipated at least a sphinx,
I wanted to learn something, I thought I could be
asked difficult questions to which the answer is
sheer presence, the cup we hold the world in, relayed
through lives, always complete. But resistance
meets nothing but resistance, on barren peat,
or the pale street-lights of a silent estate.

I feel like a NHS heart specialist who suddenly finds
that the enemy is not death but life. Lessons of the
1990s. All those slow centuries, livesful of teaching
and practice and sudden vision like a Duccio madonna,
care engineered to a working process: *de Humilitate*
gold-worked silks pressed to the ground before
the human fact – all suddenly nothing. Someone
creeps up behind you and says, 'Hey, I could sell that'
and does. Soldiers, managers, are sent into the hospital.
To break it up. They do this out of love.


Not for themselves, that's the point. It's an idea,
it's a vision. It transgresses death. But death
is always welcome. Capella Pratensis singing Josquin
in a dark church in north Holland against occasional
foghorns on the vast foggy canals, sing in the very
jaws of it, dance in a line as the happy mouth closes,
continually on an island in harm. Blood flecks on
the pillow, *ploravit in nocte*, powerless is the tenor of
the plainchant or the complex song. I'm prince of life
but I shan't be worried long.


For death is always appropriate. 'See: he has escaped
the whole thing' and lies in my arms weightless
as a college leaf, completely forgotten. But else-
where calcium and phosphor take the same chance
again, the skull grows like a midnight mushroom
in the proactive womb. What was that call he gave?
Before he left? A white shout that span across
the black fields like a furtive bride, white ribbons
on his bonny waist – hushaby child, your cradle
rocks on the hilltop, your cry calls to arms.

Meaning I depart voluntarily but for heaven's sake
do something about these holes in sense these
darknesses in the world's diction. These sombre
suits that cash any crisis as soon as. I crouch here
in bureaucratic terror like an Inca summit child
awaiting the social spasm and a motherly homunculus
in my stomach is the only messenger of history,
barking at the head carousel, saying Come down,
child, from those fancy wilds. Come to the sable
spread where what we love is asked for. For


My days are full of fear but my nights are joyous
bouts of nonentity. Unavoidable questions of value
engender the fear which twists my shoulder blades and
pushes its thumb between my eyes (have I mentioned
this symptom before?) until the kind god scoops
me up and lays me in a selfless enclosure of use-
less calm. Rocking like a beam engine in the wild
night under the windward stack what have I
to bring? I notice again that even tune whistled
below the force, as something far from this hole.


And sit up again. And shout: *Don't you know it's
bad luck to whistle in the wings during Macbeth?*
No reply, unless someone whispered *Could you
spare some small change?* In this tearing wind
I can't make out a word in this darkness I can't
distinguish a separate demand in the density of
population I can't find a home. I'd live alone
in a caravan on the edge of a Welsh field if I
believed in God. Did a voice come from a hole in
one of the stone-heaps like a song from a craft?

*You can't make a cave in that one,* I shout, *it's*
*the shaft mound! You'll burrow into nonentity.*
No answer. Is that a depth there, or merely a shade?
I lurch towards it but cyclonic pressure allies with
bronchitis: I'm silenced, lose my bearings and fall
among loose stones which rattle down, and dying to
answer can only ask: Where are you? What shall I
do next? If I locate your homelessness and dialogue
through it shall humanity in my breast bear
a lighter burden, a dawn of trust in the streets of Durban?


One thing exchanging for the other. A dawn of frost
in field and garden. You can keep your homeless
certainty, your privileged plea: I'm out here
in the entire length of land and won't be drawn back
to a social problem, I'm looking for the template error
that leads harm on through worlds without need, and
yet if I could locate your hand I would certainly
press a coin into it, if I had obtained one recently.
One thing for the other, a valid token for the touch of
recompensing flesh, and the voice it nightly manufactures.


I hear it now: Look at you, it whispers, all got up for
the fight in the hilltop pulpit and someone hands you
a note: 'Please excuse Peter from games today,
he has a slight cold and doesn't like having his face
stamped into the mud…' And rage, against the dousing
of your light in easy terms, your logic in selfish
metrics. And a messenger you can't hear, an ally
or adversary you can't locate laughs in the darkness
at the closing of the gates (of the heart. Clutch
what's left your innocence and depart.)

And go content, for actually (the whereless voice
continues) this is indeed the top tribunal, this is
what you asked for, the question at your feet. You're
not in Cambridge now – pick it up and ask it. I do.
I tick and tock under the broken stone and bid for
straight answers: *What about the lives? – if the lives mean*
*only to this limit* (tapping the surface) *what*
*completes them?* Shut up! the little sphinx murmurs,
Go away. I don't care. I want to programme quicker trains.
I want to daft us all in bigger and bigger drainage units.


It could be that I won that one, though the few plants
on the exhausted slopes quiver and cough through the night
and I hate winning anything. That was also my last chance
to mount a hilltop theatre. But I never was much
of a college kind. I was never a village fellow. I grasp
the world by its corners and shake it in the wind
which hoots over me like a new year greeting. And three
lines short of a stanza suddenly realise that the dragons
of earth are all round me. Their silence, their fear,
their no-theology, is what tears my heart to death.


For we fear the unfearable from breakfast to year's end.
I stumble to my feet grab my hapsack and slope
off under the wall. How like the populace I am,
crouched against threat, paying the lords, waiting
centuries for a democracy that never arrives, ailing
downhill sheltered from thought. The dragons of day
breathe behind the stones as I slip off the ridge-back.
I hear their piston talk, their adversarials. I fall
Down the night pleading silently for the souls
Of those who caused hurt in a rushed quest for peace.

Down the grass track, sheltering wall to right, down which
produce of that miserable bit of superseded industry
would once have been dragged by horses to line
someone's pocket or poison someone's bread and
onto the road. Even on foot tarmac quickens the pace
and like the owner of a dry-cleaning firm in Oldham
heading for a motel date I zoom down the smoothed way
as if I were going to live. I'm not. Neither is he. We both
fool ourselves into momentary eternities while
the dragons of result smoke behind our backs.


The road however soon shrinks, twists and drops,
and ejects me onto NT land below the manor house,
in which someone by luck or privilege or just possibly
rewarded labour, lives. But it is a simple place,
a valley-head junction of rounded hill-flanks with
a three-storey 17th century towerlet in grey stone
presiding over the routes thus formed at the feet
of the slopes while the working dragons cut comfort
to fillets on the far moors. And rough as it is
this tufty terrain is welcome home from such wars.


Welcome home to a fiction of rewarded labour.
But what a house to die in! What a lay-by in
which to abandon the hopeless machine and
stumble off across the fields among the slightly
interested cows begging eternity to a clay bed. Or to
wake up in the morning on the top floor and see
the white light between mullions, the snow-coated
hillsides and the telephone ringing with a message
from a daughter in Durban saying it's safe here but
something of a bore, the cars again and the hatred.

And how bright these other hills, so far from dawn,
leapfrogging before me, left of south, whose heights are
pure reason and whose flanks are crowded with earnest
surgeons whose bank accounts are the laughing-stock
of every accountant in heaven. Look at their white coats
dotted over the bounding slopes. Whose heights are
the triumph of memory in days of managing, where
cosmological princes study the lie of the land as
a strategy against harm, to the throbbing roar
of the balancing engines on the opposite moor.


These hills where there's plenty of time, you can
search all night for a stray crotchet and arise
not a whit wiser in the green morning but a
continuance to be continued a fragment fitted
to a future formulation bypassing in sufficiency
the constant failure of advantage. But exactly
fitted, exactly fair. O you black-eyed Susan,
you made me love you and left me standing here
in excess of make-believe, trying to dream
the real into a fiction in order to forget it.


A five-piece brass band appears for three seconds
across the pasture where the valley head starts to dip.
They stand on the path beside the stream, raise
their instruments to their lips, get through the first
upbeat of the Rákóczy March and vanish. It means
I can't stop, it means I can't forget, it means
two hundred years of industry brush the grasses
down the fellside. O you black-faced coalman
who dumped the earth in a heap with a crunch
and woke everyone from a dream of desert.

The glint of metal in random night. I saw
a socialist statement scissored before it
could become a nationalist sentiment. I saw
the shortest hope as the truest. *Blush Roses
in a Glass* (1905). Everything I saw vanished
and I walked on under the somnolent arcades
of night. I felt like Ivor Gurney, to whom walking
was a necessary music, audible in darkness,
eating the miles, consuming the place. Ah that!
with chips would fill my best face right now.


O you white-faced clown, blushing under the powder,
you surface of earth, where have you put my brother?
I walk into the top of the valley where the stream
comes shaking under the hill like a tizzy girl
such as I was in 1957, mincing across Manchester
to the tune of Drainpipe Shuffle (O you pink-faced
bloom you blue-bummed baboon you earthly fear,
when will you finally relinquish me to the five winds
of total forgetting?) This wayward distractedness
is entirely typical of middle-aged war-children.


Remembering the drone in the sky (you red-faced prefects,
don't you remember this?) the bombers moving in formation
towards Manchester with the concerted irrevocability
of a sextet by Lawes (William) the big grey balloons over
the houses and Death walking the bounds of the playpen.
Do you think we had need of gender remodelling?
Such wars are always with us, the old enemy and the old
fear and the shining of hearts in mutual trust,
passing mugs of tea into the bunker, setting a hand
on a shoulder, listening, listening all night long.

You listen long and eventually you hear, the
enemy approaching, the slight wind shifting
the bushes and the delicate stream beside you
chatting into gravity, the enemy earth whose
disguise is such delight. Take me by hand or
shoulder, son or daughter, and we'll walk together
down a long street or short valley decorated with
meaningful bushes. Easy walking, no harm, years
passing, I shrink as you grow. And the nearest thing
becomes the most difficult to remember, a hidden glow.


A lightness in the tread. Something happened, I
don't think we'll ever know exactly what it was
it was like casting off high culture for ever and
locating instead a common desire that shed heat
and light from the centre to the atlas index like
an anchor chain, though it wasn't exactly that either
for it was sad enough dancing on the earthen floor
so far from power; but the hope in this thought was
practical, the strictness was a far sustained voice
and the bushes this year loaded as never before.


It takes some courage, actually, to inhabit survival,
to set the burden of technology aside like a wet rucksack
or the artists with their fingers up each other's noses
and locate a human adequacy speaking only of the world,
only of the green road, green by night and green by day
that gently falls, I'm opposed to a universities poetry.
As the valley deepens, faint hint of day on the moon
coated tops, let us instead be a people, let us be
zonked out on people wine. And sing like Roza Eskenazi
of the peculiar joys of sustenance, the daily fine.

All over the fellside the bushes sing to me clad in
fruit. They sing in the night of what they learned
in the day; the lyrics are truly African: 'Education
is the only way forwards / I wanna hold your hand /
Look for peace on the gathering road my children'.
They sing variously in a choral landscape so that
an accord runs over the valley from edge to edge
and revolves with the stars like something by Obrecht,
folding and refolding on itself in the dark distances
and finally settling almost into nothing on earth.


So answering we die. But the green road continues.
It is itself the death we are in. As are the berries
hanging in great red clusters on the dry hawthorns.
As I pass down the valley each bush calls my name
and clearly states its thesis in the available space
of the night, when the light tread of the old man
walking to the sea rings out clear as a bell.
Ways of doing good in the world. I try to hear
what they say though the self-music of a proud longing
pulls me away and all the bills I'd like to pay.


Bush 18. I keep a bar down town. Get the best music,
hi-life guitar bands on tour, or some old guy up in the hills
does sanza like an angel, I get to hear and in two weeks
he's on. Local nonsense too, got to give them a chance.
I pay proper, they go on all night, people really listen.
The kids start fights but they're kids, soldiers, most
soldiers are kids, and get a good time out of any war.
The troublemakers hide from the music round corners.
We sweep up next morning. Stick my claim to virtue
on the back-wall slate: I got them singing together.

Bush 27. All I do is work in a shoe-shop and hope
one day to get married and have children, perhaps
in one of the stone-row houses in the hills I always
rather fancied that, they'd have breathing-space
and fewer temptations. I could talk to them as the rain
banged on the slates and shifted the tumblestones
down to the stream, telling them how to live, how
should I know as if I'd get bright in the brightness
and perhaps I would too. What more did you
ever do, artist, claimant? Make us a chair to die in.

Bush 32. I like to speak to the patient before I
operate and give as full an account as possible of
what I'm going to do. And afterwards I hang around,
witness the slow revival, talk, join in some basic
nursing. I won't be rushed – I have after all quite
possibly saved or extended a life or made it bearable.
I like to see it revive, that's all. The life, not the person.
What I've mended doesn't belong to the person and
my act must be understood as an episode of a work
driven into the whole world's unrolling darkness.

Bush 33. Bells on her ankles, that descant when the sun
divides. Little bird, when you've woken up and had your
breakfast, fly to her, my knot of sorrows on your back,
and remind her all her paths are peace, say a stone heart
will crack, a wax heart will melt. Then goodbye to the
circuses, goodbye to the soldiers, let a holocaust of nostalgia
and love spread all around us! Edge-being, await my message
of post-metropolitan resolution and take it to the earth's
end for her I adores, ignoring the stuffed shirt on my left.
Never could bear a successful gorse.

Bush 57. I have devoted my whole life to a careful study
and meticulous translation. I have collected and preserved
many artifacts and natural objects and have taken hundreds
of photographs of the people and the places. I have taped
the singing and notated the dancing. I have listened to them
talking and transcribed what was said into fifty manuscript
volumes. And I hope to have understood, or what could not
be understood, to have faithfully set out as it was done and said,
for the sake of a wholeness which informed everything about them.
What kept me going was the love that grew slowly towards me.


Bush 60. I cuff the kids around here about the ears. They act
as if their nose tips are the heart of hearts, come off it I say,
use your eyes. Me I never read but half a book but I know
from somewhere it's not going to work, I can see them at eighty,
pitiful relics clinging to bits of pride in the roar of death
saying I did it my way. Come off it is my answer, share
your sweets with her they can't afford them and feel the better for it
give yourself a sweet sleep. Look her in the eyes, I say, and
wallop them, you can't get too close, watch the mouth quiver.
The half book I read said something very similar.


And a good fifty others and a lot more over the next hill,
making a calling and a whispering all over the landscape
through which a fox might snake a route at ground level
or a lamb tremble under its mother's flank or a wise
southern songster cry at the vista of separation. Half
sentences and stray words torn by political advantage,
cast and lost in the night air, here and gone, fully trans-
scribed and dumped in a skip at the next library chuck-out,
and scattered to the winds. I particularly liked the Irish
shepherd who'd found a new way of squaring the circle.

And as the lost claims shoot across the small valley
they network together and make a chorus, a gathering
conditional that takes my arm like a faithful relative,
ways of doing good and the world tightens
and clarifies into a pure lament, the song the
four fairies sing at death's door: *Si je n'étais*
*pas captive, j'aimerais ce pays.* I thought I
caught it but the valley of chanting bushes comes
abruptly to an end, the last accord floats off north
I am left facing a grassed bank for all I'm worth.


I'm worth what I'm called. There's a small path
through the branches that climbs to the right,
over the bank and down some concrete steps into
the Mill yard by the tumbling water where my
lost twin waits for me. The kind compliant me I
cast adrift for the sake of upper questions and what
did I or anyone gain? A very late bush (79?) calls
over the rooftop, 'I catalogued the five joys in order,
do I get a reward?' Smile knowingly, raise
an arm and merge into each other silently.


And walk over the bridge splash across the ford and
tramp on the easy road under the cliffs – uneasily,
surrounded by dangers, but relying on common sense,
trusting in trust: somewhere the world's credit
is good and a crackling 1920s 78 from Dallas still rolls
its sad echo down the mind's question, for there are
no sureties. Virtue scrolls from eventuality. Take me
with you, Dusky Meadows, and we'll walk perpetually
in darkness dear, as I do now in darkness drear
and ever threat of error guided by own fear.

Fear of dark water. Fear of apparitions, like
a bunch of skinheads rolling down the road twirling
chains, shouting GO HOME to the homeless, ready to
pounce on the faintest glimmer of difference on
anyone's face and stamp it literally into the ground.
Safe in the knowledge of doing good, for the future,
absolutely pure. Fear of skinheads, fear of walking
into a river in the unfenced darkness when you can
hear it falling around you. Skinheads falling into
purity with big thumps. Hear the thumps and weep.


Chubby infants fallen into error, weep for them, weep
for their big trousers, the chains round their wrists,
weep for their premature baldness and loss of adventure
in ersatz certainty, weep for the bold ungiving kids they were.
I do, I worry and sob in provincial helplessness while a
financier in Leeds casually spends the night stripping
Korea of what prosperity it has. So the darkness closes
round, the valley deepens, the river sound shrinks to
a gurgle in the museum of fear I sniff to myself under
rock formations that spell dread (thump) completely clear.


I pause under an overhang, skinheads falling to earth
all round me like lambs dropped by eagles, skinheads
changing their minds and offering sweets to Slovak
gypsy children – O what a fall from ideology was that!
(thump) what loss of image what sudden and true
messages A to B in a flash of kindness, nothing is
faster, nothing more common, give the earth for it.
The eagles' nest was long deserted and the bones of
trusting lambs decorate its margins, souls intact
and speaking messages of thanks across vertical thumps.

I weep on the small winding road (far thump) and again
hear a singing somewhere. 'The musicians follow the dancers
down the main street towards dawn, playing and singing,
*My tears fall and soak my shirt, they make a pool in my lap...*'
Musicians ushering us back to our real conditions
by the morning star, drawing us out of the dream
*Autumn comes, the nights grow cold, the leaves fall off the trees,
the young men are taken into the army.* The sadness reveals
a rightness (near thump) and the cold skies watch us
making a rightness out of what we can't prevent.


But people learn, slowly. That they don't have to,
send their sons to an early grave, don't have to
live badly for the sake of the national economy.
Don't trust the music if it isn't attached, if it goes
wandering off up its own track unlikely to come back,
pirouetting on the ridge-top and leaving us helpless
at the end of the party, hopping and stumbling
back to our empty houses, from which the children
have been removed but a small flame perpetually
burns in a jar. A small flame burns in a jar.


We also get older, and mysterious bumps appear
here and there, the artists wave their nose-bags and
skinheads thumpetty-thump in the bare fields
but a small flame burns on. If it goes out here
it revives there. The old flute hangs by the hearth
waiting to be repaired, to trill out over the darkness
and burdens of sorrow like the lark in the morning
soaring and trilling above doomed farms, singing
Last night I lay in a good feather-bed, this night I lie
in a cold open field, under a gypsy laddie-O.

For this I gave up the earth, and my baby and
life itself. Full of result the virtuoso lark trills
in the sky, tied harmonically to a history of hurt.
Trills in hunger and slides and soars in fear, this
bird I cannot hear, for it is still pitch night
and no birds sing. But a dreaming murmur from
nestlings in pockets of the pale cliff says
tomorrow will be my dancing day. Tomorrow
the rights of man are reconciled with the earth
in an open field with the slim dark faithful boy.


Signalling the end of the metropolis, redundant
to communication production or distribution.
A few lost souls left dancing by themselves
to a full-blast machine-music, a few mind-suicides
on a night out. It preaches, and it threatens, it says
We shall not be moved, it waves a red flag in the
darkness but it's too late. Slowness has won.
Trees invade the centre and flourish among desks
and machines, all claims to status are so much
tinnitus and the owl mocks the benighted politician.


I know perfectly well what's going on. The river
gradually disappears into holes in its own bed
and clefts under the white cliff, with a slightly
horrible gurgle. As far as I'm concerned the whole
works goes with it, the great conurbation that never
distributed anything but despair, this is where we pull
the plug on centralist coercion and turn to each
absent other in the pitch silence, people remembered
at their best. And shake hands with that shade, welcome
the beast in its eye and the bioplast of which it's made.

The no-longer-feared stranger who pats my head and
scratches my back and pushes me on my way merrily
without saying a word, black person on dark road,
someone my daughter met in Mozambique who helped
her on her way and out of nothing gave a small meal
to two young whites… memory of days not lost, not
sad, not here. The just, who from their labours rest,
shine in the heads of poor travellers. What other reason
is there for travelling, walking the night, but to find this
justice, and the roadside constellation that carries it through?


And wouldn't so much as contemplate a war, but
fights for peace: a space in strife in which things are
born, and die, and dance, and work through a quiet
or turbulent life to further the promise into the future.
This must be what I believe in, a trust open to any-
one, in whatever text of work they operate, so long,
Babylon. And close the gate behind you. A strange
silence after the river has sunk away, lifting attention
to the top horizons and what they hold in their cryptic
script: hints of light, movement of air, final reward.


So very long, Babylon. I remember walking here
on New Year's Eve, must have been about 1977 just
after the child was born. It was well below zero and in
the frosted air the pale cliffs glowed fuzzily either
side of the dark trough in which I walked, it was
the moon's stage and my speech on it was cut.
The river was very slight and a turning point in
a life was a treaty with strife. That must be why
it sticks. Again that Senegalese singing wrecks my
business-float and the proud breeze blocks dissolve.

Lessons for others: advance cannot be virtue. Yellow
cowslips hide their heads at night and the roadside
cup-bearers keep so still the meniscus of the wine
is like glass. Advance can at best be necessity.
Some skinheads are all right actually: great lollopers,
Shropshire lads on a night out, surfers caught in
a wave they didn't propose – I've known meaner and
more vicious types on the far left, and high academe.
Uphill is where we advance from here, me & me, and fast:
the poetry police are at my back: You Been Statemented!


The road crosses the river and shoots up the hillside.
I really can't manage it, I'm almost treading the spot.
I creep the first stretch and pull myself slowly round
the corner under Thor's Cave. I can't do it, I sway
from side to side and stop laughing. The old men
dancing, that Ciarán Carson speaks of, their whole lives
stood behind them in the dance as they summed the courage
of being exactly where they were. I'm stuck. I don't know
where you are, I'm sitting on a sod in the dark facing
an inverse moon with my heart beating a different tune.


Hounds behind me, echoing their calls across the vale:
'Get the tell-tale!' and I'm stuck, a stranded whale
puffing on the verge. My failure to climb this hill
is the funniest thing and the moon sails on the sill
of my heart, casting brightness to the night sky, lost
into space. And there, receiving the acclaim of the host
of distances, Thor's Cave lords it over me, who can only
fall to the edge and laugh at his weakness. It could be
I have hidden reserves, it could be my entire history
is drawn to a hole in the sky for what it deserves.

Teach me to see, hollow eye, to hear, blocked tube,
into the distances that hold the solution to fear,
an arm round a poor man's shoulder, a widower
in the scents of night, the rustling broom on the
sloping roadside. A listening trumpet that calls
into the far reaches of the climate messages of
wholeness the far earth turns towards, setting
a cloak of aromatic air on a poor man's shoulder
whose bad eye sees the furthest and whose waxy ear
catches an echo in the rustle, pronouncing a name.


Names change from time to time. I breathe one in and
prise myself to my feet, I must continue. I nod to
the cave in the sky, lord of the heavy sentence whose
trumpet blasts anger over from the industrial estates,
silent at night under needless street lamps. The anger
challenges a long succession of undeserved gain
for the sake of the labourers whose loss makes
the entire dictionary, whose loss is continual. For my
heart is always trembling, from clear day light to dawn,
at the warnings that must stay silent


And the loves that must fail. Person much missed, how
you call to me in the capitalised pause and your
scattered ashes float above me like patches of mist
on the dark slopes drawing me up the hill. The night
collapses nightly into this loss, and someone has to
walk it into day through the dark of dreams, scratch
the writing across the sloping desk-top over the
furrows and ink pits. Much missed person my hope
is always there where my heart's capital is sunk.
See it through, I tell myself, to the end of the book.

And I no longer hear that music, that partialises the world
and the rich silence I hear instead specifically lacks any
call, any claim or region. Yet your story made all these
hills and how wonderful it would be to hear a few bars of
S.E. Rogie's sweet baritone voice singing 'Nodomei Neneckpa'
the sweetest, most beautiful, powerful thing: singing
simply, there is a best thing. The comfort needed
at waking because we know the night gap has been
betrayed again. I wonder where you are tonight don't
pass me by don't spill the sky's translucent wine.


Or the soaring contralto of Munadjat Yulchieva holding
all our answers to unkind fate, our sky clothes, our
few night jewels. And the birds have already heard
the news and are passing it on. From tree and bush
in barely a trace of light the old questions are beginning
to be asked, high up the throat, What chance now?
What choice? Are you still there? Do you remember
Caruso at Belle Vue in 1953? Yes, every turn every
restitution every final farewell, nothing is lost.
It all gathers to the great chorus of hunger.


The best thing, but all I can think is complete thing,
get up this murderous hill under the frown of
judge rock with hole for face get this night over:
step step inch inchworm cold pre-dawn when human
tide is lowest, might be. Forgotten why, forgotten what,
working/walking, for. Left (over) poetry forgotten.
And good riddance, however many or few human
souls gather at the river one day we'll cross over
and not be disappointed. True expectation, of
astral liquor, exactly where we succeed.

The road eases between banks (flesh crumbles into dust)
pace quickens, head back again (Dies Fleisch, das
in den Staub zerfällt) up onto the plateau the fields
edged in dull stone the dust brewed into humus. Tod!
Wo ist dein Stachel? Usefulness is freedom and here's me,
travelling on, rich in a currency nobody recognises
and quite prepared to chuck the whole (whatever it
was) enterprise over my shoulder (Dein Sieg, o Hölle!
Wo ist er? / Unser ist der Sieg) like a hibernating toad
but I have gone the wrong way and there's a knight in the road.


I went on towards Wetton turned south in the sleepy
fieldsides to get round to the Alstonefield road
and it was normal except when Shostakovich's head
suddenly popped over a wall saying, 'Furthermore,
every time they play me now they preach about Stalin
as if that's what the whole thing was about. All I
wanted was to forget Stalin…' but it seemed the music
had forgotten me and all the trouble in the world when I
found myself at Long Low, desolate and cold, where
hope meets pain and I think there's a knight in the road.


I was walking on with my head full and noticed after
a while the road was getting very dusty and developed
a central grass ridge, sure sign of impending impasse
and it began to seem to look quite likely to me that
this road was the wrong road, that it led to where
I didn't want to get to or indeed didn't lead to
anywhere at all but stopped at a field gate and
a sense of death as failure, as everyone's own indi-
vidual failure to continue, as a relinquishment of
energy and purpose and a knight in the road saying so.

In, actually, some light now, some pre-dawn squabble.
Out here at the end of the road where the gods hide
behind the field-walls and watch their monuments:
'battlefields to the right, hospitals to the left', another
abandoned mine following a vein towards the valley
edge, heaps and holes; and to the left a linear tumulus
unique in Britain. These lines cross my path and I
stand alone in a mitigated darkness still bound up in
stillness save for the groaning birds the wind and
the heaviness of the load for there's that knight in the road.


False knight in false dawn, like a gibbet by the track.
*You sought your self.* My head hurts, I can't breathe
properly. *What's that you're carrying?* I don't want
to go to school, the teacher's got it in for me, I try my
best but I miss the questions. *It's a teddy-bear isn't it.*
It's late, I'm going home, everyone will still be there.
*Nothing you do, nothing you say.* I just wanted to pass by
I just wanted to die. *I don't see that there's any alternative*
*to a constant strengthening against the powers of this world*
*and any who can't/won't is a lost life I haven't the time*


*For, falling. The world falls and you jump on board*
*you share the world's lapse but it doesn't lapse half*
*enough for me with you heartening it. It was bad enough*
*and now there's you too, humaning it back into time,*
*selling itself for a song. Look how wetly it glints in its*
*wrapping, this you-world. I won't have it here I'll thwart it*
*out of you I'll stop your eyes where it lurks smiling —*
*right back in there it lurks, your love of all this, being.*
*Take your pet and go. Go failed, go subdued, go weak,*
*go self-blamed and go now.* I'd like to say three things.

(1) Hard falls the rain on the lip that bites its owner.
(2) What is anyone ever going to make in this place
but a brooch of honour in the covering darkness,
an ornament passed to a future friend? (3) You may be
right but at least I never prioritised resentment.
He's gone. Was it a he? It vanished downwards with a
hollow tone, I'm alone at the road's end and the stories
that made these hung fields hollow me out like a bell,
like a churchyard bell calling the gods to their hunger.
They are hungry for the day and shadow me wherever I wander.


At the road's end you turn round and go back home
but I stand here in acute smallness, a life spent in
a dream of verbal redemption while the *polis* fingers me.
Something, not a bat, flits from the mine ruins back
to the passage grave. The steel-grey fields wrap both
of them in shopping, in slumber, in healthy tissue.
Nothing moves. These scars, heaps, works, these long
forgotten stories, these accusations, stand there like
tanks by the roadside and a small bird makes for cover
with a quick flutter. We must stand by our own stories.


Halted at almost-dawn far but not so very far away
and certainly still within privilege. In eastern border-
zones centuries of failed diplomacy continue to blast
shells into living-rooms and every night is a question
of waking. The peace and mind-spaces we enjoy here
were hard won and rare on the earth, at a price of distraction
and disappointment. The mind runs on its vocabulary
to the end of the road, what it finds there is a shadow
of itself, no use blaming the government if it runs guilt into
our living space. The harm done is actual and irreparable.

The grey fields barely emerging into visibility,
the laying of diffused water on the land, the leaves
throwing open their shutters and switching on
the radio for the morning news: distant stories,
threats and promises, all quietly. And moving into
the calmed land, not yet measured by work. Some-
where the maidens dance on the green at break of day
arm in arm in a ring and nothing from an idea to
a tubercular lung can break that tuneful process
or mitigate the pain that showers final light on those subtly


Deferring messengers. Final dark is dimmed indeed as I
follow the way the tall sign points, down the grassy fields
on the stile path to Hope Dale brushing the dew and
the singing accumulates from hidden quarters as the colour
fills in, shadows retreating before me and the birds all
up in arms. There by the lower pond and up across
the fallow slopes the backs of soldiers under instruction
to silently vanish from sight shrink into the darkness
that clings to corners. Armies in retreat with their new
recruits and the long wedding is over, the band follows


The last revellers down the road singing *My tears fall
and soak my shirt*, the early wind breaks little hollows
in the hedgerows and pastures and the leaves flit past us
as we make our way back to our quiet houses. To sleep
and be ill, and retch up mucus from the lung, and
call it a day, forgetting our children's names. Blanked
by the music, like Amédé Ardoin, one of my heroes,
who lay by a railroad track in Louisiana punished for
serving, punished for fidelity and never knew another
thing never played another note and called it living hell.

And got out fast. Which is a long way to go with the songs
of longing beating in your head and the accordion for ever
removed from your hands. I go on over the tumbling
peneplain, the road mounting humps and scooping hollows,
shadows everywhere departing, red lights on their bumpers.
Back of night or receding armies, creeping along hedgerows
clutching trophies. That man who sang out sweet and plain
is no longer on the circuits. But his answer cruises strife
and strolls from the known to its fore edges. *He do the song
about the night. He do the walk, he do the walk of life.*


Excuse me sir have you got a licence for that singing
says politely a police voice behind me I'd forgotten all
about. I know nothing of this I was brought here against
my will and stuff my mascot under my blazer as the tall
trees call their laws over. But I'd like to say three things:
(4) They are working people, the musicians and plasterers
who guide us back to where we live in a dawn halo
of old and tried devices – see how they walk with their
consorts on the sweet paths of earnest learning and learnèd
earning. You who die be my compass this curling morn.


A young woman in a nurses' uniform leaves one of
the scattered cottages, gets into a car, the first car, and
drives off towards Hulme End. A sleep-over, an old man
dying of lung cancer, a daughter. I wish I had been
like you and never tendered the artistic excuse. But to be
even in this thin light a working agent and the very ground,
the dawning territory itself, is won back. Back from what?
Sleep and adventure. To what? The real. These failed
missionaries in black robes running under the road's
edge from day are but your dwarfs and do what you say.

I'd like to say three things: (1) Where does such
tenderness come from? As I pass by Hope the
singular thing pours, the morning star, the lark
on high. There it goes, like Nusrat Fateh Ali Khan
on one of his shaking ascents and the sign of
tomorrow is a fat man shrinking into the sky,
rising into the precise location of a known star.
Cold mornings, it's autumn, the leaves fall from
the trees, the young men are taken into the army,
half of them never come back, the bark of care.


I wish I were entering a land. Rattle of the death-
camps in the stream-bed, carried away – a music
you can't have or bear back home, you can't
have it, they say, it remains ours. He don't say
nothin, he just keep. He roll. I gets weary.
Water clocks in the sky, little owls in the trees,
shadows of dispersing armies. I thought I heard
in the swift dawn air a nursing person shouting angrily
at the ideological accusers that segregate our band.
I wanted to live, she said, in a land.


And you shall, I thought, coming up the slope into
Alstonefield, still sleeping. And passed along
the deserted street to the starting point, the village
football pitch to the left of the road, site of the
boot sale and what I collapse into isn't the B & B
which I never booked myself back to anyway, but the
cheap red car in the village car-park. Soon the farmworkers
will be out in those mobile telephone booths spreading
hip-hop music on the land. The earth's movement never
stops. I've had enough of this, I want a record shop.

Yet the laying of stone on stone, the careful nurturing
of pot plants in a lean-to, are as much signs that people
find life worth having and are prepared to do something
with, in, by, and for it, any day. Let's call it a day –
a tired man motionless in a car thinking feeble thoughts.
Where are you going, dove, this pale wine
of new day? Bundle of nerve calling over the slates
and pausing on the wires as the echoes conjoin, where
are you off to now? I'm going right out of this world,
and I'm taking your love with me.

# Notes

## Preface

**p. 2** Estimate Brown (not to be confused with either Capability Brown or Shallow Brown): John Brown, 1715–66, writer of essays and guide-books, early promoter of the enjoyment of wild mountain scenery, influenced Wordsworth.

ringed in darkness: the Peak District is encompassed on three sides by (a) gritstone moorlands to west, north and east, producing landscape of a darker hue, (b) large industrial or ex-industrial conurbations from north-east clockwise to north-west: Sheffield, Nottingham, Derby, Stoke-on-Trent, Manchester.


## Part I

**p. 6** distances steeped in petrol: I have established experimentally that it is impossible anywhere in the Peak District, even in the middle of the night, to get away from the sound of the internal combustion engine for any length of time – near at hand, beyond the horizon, or in the sky.

Mansfield: town on the Derbyshire–Nottinghamshire border to the east, ex-coal mining area now depressed. It was said to be a centre for small-time British fascism.


## Part II

**p. 9** The sky will not help you...: from one of Martin Luther's sermons.

**p. 12** Thor's lip: reference to Thor's Cave in the Manifold Valley, which is passed again in Part V. It is a large water-worn, indeed whirlpool-worn cave, and looks it, but is perched on the very summit of the valley side, as the stratum in which it was formed has shifted thither in geological time.

miner's hammer: there are traces of former metal mining in the Alstonefield area but the sense of a palace under your feet shining with galena (crystalline lead ore) is imported from the eastern side of the Peak District.

**p. 12**  Lulu: a popular singer in the late 1960s. She never, to my knowledge, did a song called 'April Fever'; nor did anybody else.

## Part III

**p. 15**  Beresford: Beresford Dale, on the River Dove upstream of Dovedale, on the edge of land which used to lie within the estate of Charles Cotton of Beresford Hall and still contains (inaccessibly) the stone fishing lodge used by him and Isaac Walton, author of *The Compleat Angler* (1653).

The coal tit, dyed in modern philosophy: black and white head above a grey-brown body.

**p. 16**  a more demanding geology: at the top of Beresford Dale the river passes from a sandstone inlier (open and gently undulating countryside) to carboniferous limestone (a gorge cut through white rock).

## Part IV

**p. 20**  Wolfscote: long tall open dale of the Dove Valley north of Alstonefield, and hill of the same name above it. Occurs several times later.

walkers' autobahn: long stretches of the riverside path in the Dove Valley now take the form of evenly laid beaten gravel about two metres wide.

Harecops: isolated Georgian stone farmhouse on the ridge of land between the Dove and Manifold valleys, with a view towards Wolfscote Hill, inhabited by the author and his family for four years in the 1970s. It is passed again rather more slowly in the middle of Part V.

## Part V

**p. 23**  Pea Low: locally to the Peak District 'low' means a rise of ground, usually a prehistoric tumulus (Old English *hlaw*).

distressed: I use this as a bookseller's term meaning 'in poor condition'.

**p. 24**  north: towards Sheffield and the gritstone moors of the Pennines.

**p. 25**  west: towards Stoke-on-Trent, possibly the grimiest, the least modernised, and the most splintered by development of the industrial conurbations around the Peak.

**p. 25**   east: towards Lincoln, for instance, but a medieval presence is generally more apparent in eastern England than in other parts.

**p. 26**   But I did, I went south: refers to the author's removal from central Derbyshire to Cambridge in 1982 – strictly south-east, but this would constitute 'going south' to a northerner.

the former sheep: the sheep mentioned when passing this point near the end of Part III, probably all lamb chops by now.

**p. 27**   The path begins to dip: the speaker has walked from the village towards the Bed & Breakfast house which is on the road out of Alstonefield to the east, then taken a footpath to the left which goes over the fields and at this point descends abruptly into Dovedale. He then walks upstream on the riverside path.

**p. 28**   Cunning little vixen: no reference to Janáček's opera, which is not really called that anyway. Similarly, 'Manchester Sonatas' does not refer to Vivaldi. The image of Manchester on the few occasions it occurs in the poem could be related to a particular period, say 1955–65, when the city was particularly distressed by both dereliction and development. It is a handy personal referent for what happened to the northern cities in general.

**p. 30**   hoquetting: musical term, from the French for 'hiccup' – a sequence of tones constantly passed from one singer to another, in its simplest form a melody using two tones in which each of two singers only ever sings one of them.

**p. 33**   *basso continuo*: the supporting bass line of seventeenth- and eighteenth-century European music, with chord structures above it indicated mathematically.

*scordatura*: the practice of changing the tuning of (especially) the violin for special effect.

*rilievo schiaccito*: extremely shallow relief engraving on stone, as practised in the Italian Quattrocento.

**p. 34**   Palazzo del Capitano dei Populi (and similar names): a kind of medieval Italian town hall, signifying self-government, republicanism and democracy. The Piazza del Popolo would be the square in front of it.

**p. 36**   My toy, my dump: both of these are also the names of instrumental musical forms current in late sixteenth-century England – short, dance-like, entertainment pieces, the latter quite sardonic.

A cobbler his wife and seven children...: Frank i'th' Rocks Cave, between Wolfscote Dale and Beresford Dale. The cobbler is mentioned in several local guidebooks.

**p. 40**   In cielo circo...: in the sky / in heaven / I seek your happy-making face. A lost quotation.

**p. 43** Elaine Scarry: in her book *The Body in Pain* (OUP, 1985).

O Delvig, Delvig: a foreboding of Shostakovich, quoting the title and incipit of the ninth song of his Symphony No. 14. The poem, by Wilhelm Küchelbeker (b. 1797) is addressed to Baron Anton Antonovich Delvig (d. 1831; both were members of Pushkin's circle) and to quote the translation accompanying the CD, 'asks what reward an artist may expect among villains and fools, castigating the power of tyrants and praising the immortality of brave deeds and art that loves freedom'. (Deutsche Grammophon 437 785-2, Gothenburg Symphony Orchestra conducted by Neeme Järvi.)

**p. 45** jack-snipes: this bird sometimes emits a strange 'drumming' sound in flight, which is not vocal but produced by the tail-feathers; it will do it at nightfall and the sound can seem to come from the air all round you.

Reverdy, Pierre: French poet whose work is marked for me by a sense that nothing is ever entirely satisfactory or makes sense, and the unending quest to know why.

**p. 47** Shallow Brown: title and refrain of a sea shanty, extant in many different versions, the gist amounting in some to 'You're going to leave me', and in others, 'I'm going to leave her'.

**p. 48** Luchistaya zvezda…: translated in the next three lines. Russian version of Michelangelo, 'Dante', set by Shostakovich as the sixth of his Suite on Verses of Michelangelo, Opus 145a.

**p. 49** tomorrow is my wedding day…: from a text set by Percy Grainger as a wedding cantata for himself.

the big stone house: Harecops, noted in Part IV.

**p. 50** quis dabit…: Which gives peace to the frightened population.

Hell-hound at the crossroads: a Delta blues trope, used for instance by Robert Johnson.

**p. 51** Where does such tenderness come from?: 'Otkúda takáya néznost?', Marina Tsvetayeva, the second of the six of her poems set by Shostakovich in his Opus 143a.

**p. 53** Archford Moor: the walker has now crossed the watershed between the Dove and Manifold valleys and is descending to meet the River Manifold at Westside Mill. On Archford Moor, see Roy Fisher's poem 'The Slink' and my comments on it in *News for the Ear: a homage to Roy Fisher* (ed. Peter Robinson and Robert Sheppard, Stride, 2000).

**p. 54** original orthography: of the church anthem by Thomas Tallis: 'If ye love me, keep my commandements, and I will pray the Father, and he shall give you another comforter, that he may bide with you for ever, e'en the sprit of truth… '

**p. 58**  artisans of Zaïre: refers not to Zaïrean commercial pop, but to ex-tribal amateur urban music for celebrations patronised by the poorer and more recently urbanised groups. See *Musiques Urbaines à Kinshasa* issued by Ocora Records, France 1986.

Apes Tor: the rock formation at the northern point of Ecton Hill (see note on p. 59). The imagery of falling water derives from the fact that there is a large mineshaft in a cave here at road level (now concreted over, walled-in and double-barred because you can't trust anybody these days not to fling themselves down a mineshaft and cause everybody a lot of trouble and the country a lot of expense). Formerly a conduit brought running water to here from a reservoir further up the west side of the hill (mentioned later) which fell down the shaft to work the waterwheels of an underground pumping engine. So falling water was employed to raise water. The shaft is just across the road from the River Manifold which for some reason was not harnessed for this purpose.

Seán 'ac Donncha: singer from Connemara, in the style known as *sean nós*, an elaborately ornamented solo singing.

**p. 59**  Ecton: the two figures into which the narrator now divides go one each side of Ecton Hill, a ridge-shaped end of high ground in the western edge of the Peak limestone, and meet up again at Wetton Mill further down the Manifold Valley. Ecton Hill was formerly one of the biggest copper mines in Europe and is riddled with underground spaces as a result of this, its surface scattered with mine ruins, spoil heaps, shaft tops and tunnel entrances, most of them now absorbed by age into the hill's worn and bleak aspect, since the mines all closed before the twentieth century.

**p. 60**  I follow the river: from here until further notice the voice is that of the one who takes the road to the right, and walks down river along the foot of Ecton Hill.

folding: horizontal rock strata folded by geological action into acute V or zig-zag shapes such as are exposed at the north end of Ecton Hill.

adits: horizontal tunnels driven into the hillside to reach the copper ores.

**p. 61**  Dorze: not another pygmy tribe but one in Ethiopia, also given to polyphonic singing.

copper spire: there is an eccentric stone house with a copper spire pushed into the side of Ecton Hill just here, built for the owner or manager of the copper mines.

**p. 62**  bureaucratic directive: at a number of road junctions in the Peak Park there are signs intended for touring visitors, which send you to the next village by the most circuitous possible route.

**p. 63**  Dead miners carolling under the hill: when Vaughan Williams took down what has become known as the Corpus Christi Carol from a Mr Hall of Castleton, Derbyshire, in about 1900, he was told that every Christmas Eve the lead miners of Castleton would descend to the lowest part of the mine, and in an open space there set a candle on a piece of lead ore, and sing the carol sitting round it in a circle.

**p. 64** high as kites: charcoal-burning produces narcotic fumes which are said to have been one of the few delights of the life of a charcoal-burner.

I asked one of these blacks…: spoken by a freedman to J. McKim c. 1850, quoted in *Negro Slave Songs in the United States*, by M.M. Fisher (Cornell, 1953).

**p. 65** *She nurst him back*…: another lost quotation. It could be from one of the female-cabin-boy songs, except that it doesn't seem to be in lyric metre.

**p. 66** Lemady: title and addressee of an English traditional song, one of those (like the previous) set by Benjamin Britten. There are several other phrases from mostly well-known English songs in the three stanzas of which this is the third.

**p. 67** tempiettos: I understand this word (which occurs again later) to mean a small temple or chapel or a model of one. The famous one is that by Bramante at S. Pietro in Montorio, Rome, which is a circular memorial chapel in a courtyard.

**p. 69** Leaving the door ajar: it is obvious that the speaker from this point onwards is the other of the two selves into which the protagonist divided at Apes Tor, and the scene returns to that point, taking a route on the other (western) side of Ecton Hill.

little lake: the reservoir for the Apes Tor shaft detailed earlier. The wooden fishing lodge at its corner was of course added after it fell into disuse.

**p. 70** Fretwork: name of a currently active viol consort.

William Lawes: English musician in the court of Charles I.

**p. 71** On this side the hill remains sealed: there are no horizontal or inclined tunnel-entrances to the mines on the western side. Due to the disposition of the metallic veins they are all on the other side.

**pp. 71–2** gather ye rose-buds…: Herrick; 'I'll tell ye what befell me…' is adapted from his 'How Lillies Came White' as set by William Lawes.

**p. 72** On the top is a mine ruin: I have not discovered the name of this mine but of all the remains on Ecton it is the one which still stands out from the surrounding terrain, with bright ungrassed stone heaps, on the shoulder of the ridge-top.

**p. 73** *The Triumph of Time and Truth*: an early oratorio by Handel (1707), originally Italian. In the English version (1757) the final chorus of Act

II begins 'Ere to dust is changed thy beauty, Change thy heart and love pursue'. It is a short four-part fugue, and a quite perfect thing.

**p. 73** Beaker posture: tightly crouched, knees to chin, like the inhumation burials of the British early Bronze Age 'Beaker' stratum, commonly interpreted as foetal.

**p. 74** *What have you to show…*: adapted from an old coal miners' song.

**p. 76** *de Humilitate*: Madonna de Humilitate – one of the formats of Virgin and Child paintings in medieval Italy, showing Mary kneeling on the ground before the baby Jesus.

Capella Pratensis: Dutch choir specialising in fifteenth-century continental liturgical music, the only one I know of which sings grouped together in front of one full-size choirbook (Pratensis: of the fields, as in Josquin Despres). (Plorans) ploravit in nocte: (She) weeping weepeth sore in the night, Lamentations I.ii. The tenor in this music is not only the voice of that pitch, but also the part which holds the polyphonic texture together by intoning in long notes the chant upon which the music is built.

white ribbons on his bonny waist: marriage or betrothal tokens, as in the song 'The trees they grow so high'.

**p. 78** *it's the shaft mound*: a mound of rocks cast up around the mouth of the vertical mineshaft itself, the top of which will now be concealed somewhere within it.

Durban: this town in South Africa occurs again later and should be taken, with all its conditions, as circumstantial (i.e. where the author's daughter happened to be at the time).

**p. 81** Rákóczy March: this would be Berlioz's version, and the band probably Salvation Army. The march itself, said to have been composed by the gypsy musician János Bihary, was a rallying-point of the nineteenth-century Hungarian struggle for independence from Austria.

**p. 82** *Blush Roses in a Glass*: painting by Fantin-Latour, in the Fitzwilliam Museum, Cambridge.

**p. 83** Roza Eskenasi (c. 1895–1980): singer of Greek–Turkish urban popular songs (*rembetika*), mainly active in the 1930s.

**p. 84** sanza: West African term for the mbira or thumb-piano.

**p. 85** tumblestones: a coinage of Barry MacSweeney.

**p. 87** *Si je n'étais pas captive…*: Victor Hugo, *La Captive*, set by Berlioz, Opus 12. 'If I were not a prisoner, I would like this country…'.

**p. 89** The musicians follow the dancers…: this and the following references in this stanza and later are from the Hungarian-speaking population of Transylvania, and refer to the 'dawn songs' which used to be sung with full instrumental accompaniment to mark the end of a night-long festivity, sometimes, as described here, as a feature of a procession back to home and normality. The words of these songs are invariably profoundly sad.

**p. 92**   Ciarán Carson: in his book on Irish music, *Last Night's Fun* (Cape, 1996).

**p. 93**   For my heart is always trembling…: these words seem to be sung by Joe Heaney in a rendition of 'The Rocks of Bawn'.

Person much missed…: adapted from Thomas Hardy, 'The Voice' (*Satires of Circumstance*).

**p. 94**   S.E. Rogie: 'palm wine' singer and guitarist from Sierra Leone who settled in England and died in about 1995.

Munadjat Yulchieva: singer from Uzbekistan.

Caruso: the Italian operatic tenor died in 1921, so the memory is an error. The tenor heard in Manchester was probably Beniamino Gigli (1890–1957).

Belle Vue: former pleasure grounds in south Manchester which included a large circular hall used for recitals, concerts, circuses, etc.

**p. 95**   Dies Fleisch, das in den Staub…: and other German in this stanza, is from the text (by Karl Wilhelm Ramler) of the oratorio *Die Auferstehung und Himmelfart Jesu*, by Carl Philip Emanuel Bach. 'This flesh that crumbles into dust…', 'Death, where is thy sting?', 'Thy victory, O Hell, where is it? Ours is the victory'.

a knight in the road: cf. the ancient ballad called by Francis James Child 'The Fause Knight upon the Road', No. 3 in his collection of 1882.

**p. 98**   Amédé Ardoin: Louisiana Cajun musician, died 1941 in an asylum, possibly as the long-term result of a violent racial attack after a dance during which, being very hot, he accepted the gift of a handkerchief from a white girl to mop his brow.

**p. 99**   *He do the song about the night*…: Dire Straits, 'Walk of Life' (known to me in a swamp pop cover version by Charles Mann).

**p. 100**   Nusrat Fateh Ali Khan: Pakistani devotional musician, Qawalli singer.

He don't say nothin…: imperfect reminiscence of the song 'Old Man River', from the musical *Show Boat*, which was mounted by Stockport Amateur Operatic Society in about 1953.

I want a record shop: a reminiscence of a poem by Frank O'Hara.